ACCA

F3/FFA FINANCIAL ACCOUNTING

REVISION ESSENTIALS

For Examinations from September 2017 to August 2018

BECKER
PROFESSIONAL EDUCATION®

For more information about any of Becker's materials, please visit our website at www.becker.com/acca or email acca@becker.com.

CONTENTS

(i)

CONTENTS

CONTENTS

CAUTION: These notes offer guidance on key issues.
Reliance on these alone is insufficient to pass the examination.

(iii)

Aim

To develop knowledge and understanding of the underlying principles and concepts relating to financial accounting and technical proficiency in the use of double-entry accounting techniques including the preparation of basic financial statements.

Main capabilities

On successful completion, candidates should be able to:

✓ explain the context and purpose of financial reporting;

✓ define qualitative characteristics of financial information;

✓ demonstrate use of double-entry and accounting systems;

✓ record transactions and events;

✓ prepare a trial balance (including identifying and correcting errors);

✓ prepare basic financial statements for incorporated and unincorporated entities;

✓ prepare simple consolidated financial statements;

✓ interpret financial statements.

Position in the overall ACCA qualification

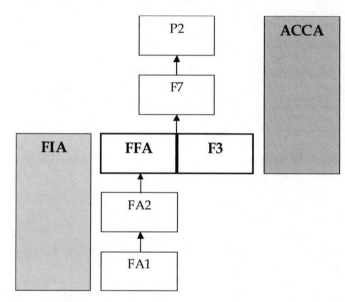

Approach to examining

ACCA Examination

- ✓ A 2 hour paper-based or computer-based examination (CBE).
- ✓ Section A: 35 two-mark objective questions ("MCQs")
- ✓ Section B: two 15-mark multi-task questions ("MTQs").
  - ➢ Consolidations (may include interpretation)
  - ➢ Accounts preparation (for sole trader or limited company)
- ✓ Both computational and non-computational elements.

Examinable documents

From 1st September 2017 until 31st August 2018

IAS 1	*Presentation of Financial Statements*
IAS 2	*Inventories*
IAS 7	*Statement of Cash Flows*
IAS 10	*Events after the Reporting Period*
IAS 16	*Property, Plant and Equipment*
IAS 27	*Separate Financial Statements*
IAS 28	*Investments in Associates*
IAS 37	*Provisions, Contingent Liabilities and Contingent Assets*
IAS 38	*Intangible Assets*
IFRS 3	*Business Combinations*
IFRS 10	*Consolidated Financial Statements*
IFRS 15	*Revenue from Contracts with Customers*
Other	
	Conceptual Framework for Financial Reporting

CORE TOPICS

CORE TOPICS	Tick when completed		Tick when completed
✓ Main elements of financial reports	☐	✓ Incomplete records	☐
✓ Classifying elements of financial statements	☐	✓ Regulatory framework	☐
✓ Accounting systems	☐	✓ Conceptual Framework	☐
✓ Book-keeping principles	☐	✓ Presentation of financial statements	☐
✓ Ledger accounting	☐	✓ Capital structure and finance costs	☐
✓ Sales and purchases	☐	✓ IAS 2 *Inventories*	☐
✓ Trial balance	☐	✓ IAS 18 *Revenue*	☐
✓ Accruals and prepayments	☐	✓ IAS 16 *Property, Plant and Equipment*	☐
✓ Depreciation and disposals	☐	✓ IAS 38 *Intangible Assets*	☐
✓ Receivables and payables	☐	✓ IAS 37 *Provisions and Contingencies*	☐
✓ Inventory (accounting)	☐	✓ IAS 10 *Events After the Reporting Period*	☐
✓ Books of prime entry	☐	✓ IAS 7 *Statements of Cash Flows*	☐
✓ Control accounts and reconciliations	☐	✓ Consolidated financial statements	☐
✓ Bank reconciliations	☐	✓ Interpretation of financial statements	☐
✓ Suspense accounts	☐		

CONTENTS

CONTENTS

CAUTION: These notes offer guidance on key issues.
Reliance on these alone is insufficient to pass the examination.

Approach to examining

ACCA Examination

- ✓ A 2 hour paper-based or computer-based examination (CBE).

- ✓ Section A: 35 two-mark objective questions ("MCQs")

- ✓ Section B: two 15-mark multi-task questions ("MTQs").

  - ➤ Consolidations (may include interpretation)
  - ➤ Accounts preparation (for sole trader or limited company)

- ✓ Both computational and non-computational elements.

Examinable documents

From 1ˢᵗ September 2017 until 31ˢᵗ August 2018

IAS 1	*Presentation of Financial Statements*
IAS 2	*Inventories*
IAS 7	*Statement of Cash Flows*
IAS 10	*Events after the Reporting Period*
IAS 16	*Property, Plant and Equipment*
IAS 27	*Separate Financial Statements*
IAS 28	*Investments in Associates*
IAS 37	*Provisions, Contingent Liabilities and Contingent Assets*
IAS 38	*Intangible Assets*
IFRS 3	*Business Combinations*
IFRS 10	*Consolidated Financial Statements*
IFRS 15	*Revenue from Contracts with Customers*
Other	
	Conceptual Framework for Financial Reporting

1 ENTITIES

1.1 Types

- ✓ Sole trader ("self-employed")
  - ➤ Controls, manages and owns business.
  - ➤ Legally, person and business are same.
  - ➤ Bears all financial risks.

- ✓ Partnership ("self employed)
  - ➤ 2+ people.
  - ➤ Profits shared by agreement.

- ✓ Incorporated ("Company")
  - ➤ Separate legal entity.
  - ➤ Owned by shareholders.
  - ➤ Run by appointed directors.
  - ➤ Subject to company law.

Simple

Complex

1.2 Sole trader

- ✓ Obliged to keep records:
  - ➤ personal transactions
  - ➤ apportion business/private use of assets.

- ✓ Wholly liable for debts, etc.

Advantages

- ✓ Almost complete control.
- ✓ Low administration costs.
- ✓ Few legal requirements.

Disadvantages

- ✗ All personal assets at risk. Risk of bankruptcy.

1.3 Partnership

- ✓ Obligations as for a sole trader.

- ✓ Liabilities – as for a sole trader but shared **jointly** (even if profits not equal).

Advantages

- ✓ More money can usually be raised for start-up.
- ✓ Few legal requirements.
- ✓ Workload can be shared.

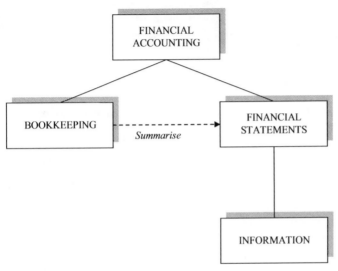

3 FINANCIAL STATEMENTS

3.1 Components

✓ Statement of financial position ("SoFP").

✓ Statement of profit or loss and other comprehensive income ("statement of comprehensive income" – SoCI):

  ➢ statement of profit or loss ("income statement");
  ➢ other comprehensive income (e.g. gains and losses).

✓ Statement of changes in equity ("SoCIE").

✓ Statement of cash flows ("CFS").

✓ Accounting policies and explanatory notes.

Non-financial statements

✓ May be included in annual report (e.g. Chairman's/ directors' statements, environmental reports, etc).

2.2 Bookkeeping

✓ "Systematic recording of financial transactions of a business".

✓ Purpose – to record every financial transaction.

✓ Activities:

  ➢ Collecting/recording of transactions (daily)
  ➢ Collating/summarizing/balancing (e.g. monthly)
  ➢ Making year-end adjustments.

1 ENTITIES

1.1 Types

- ✓ Sole trader ("self-employed")
  - ➢ Controls, manages and owns business.
  - ➢ Legally, person and business are same.
  - ➢ Bears all financial risks.

- ✓ Partnership ("self employed)
  - ➢ 2+ people.
  - ➢ Profits shared by agreement.

- ✓ Incorporated ("Company")
  - ➢ Separate legal entity.
  - ➢ Owned by shareholders.
  - ➢ Run by appointed directors.
  - ➢ Subject to company law.

Simple

Complex

1.2 Sole trader

- ✓ Obliged to keep records:
  - ➢ personal transactions
  - ➢ apportion business/private use of assets.

- ✓ Wholly liable for debts, etc.

Advantages

- ✓ Almost complete control.
- ✓ Low administration costs.
- ✓ Few legal requirements.

Disadvantages

- ✗ All personal assets at risk. Risk of bankruptcy.

1.3 Partnership

- ✓ Obligations as for a sole trader.

- ✓ Liabilities – as for a sole trader but shared **jointly** (even if profits not equal).

Advantages

- ✓ More money can usually be raised for start-up.

- ✓ Few legal requirements.

- ✓ Workload can be shared.

Disadvantages

✘   Risk of personal bankruptcy.

✘   Need for joint decisions may hamper business.

✘   Potential for conflict $\Rightarrow$ risk.

1.4   Limited company

Obligations

✓   Must hold an Annual General Meeting (AGM):

     ➢   to receive/approve Annual Reports
     ➢   to appoint directors and auditors.

✓   To meet legal filing requirements.

✓   To have at least one director.

✓   In UK (for example) to have a company secretary.

Liabilities

✓   To taxation (on all profits).
✓   Share capital determines limit of shareholders' liability.

Advantages

✓   Directors protected from legal actions (if act in good faith).

Disadvantages

✘   Much more administration.
✘   Director has employee status (may be tax disadvantages).
✘   Business affairs not private.

2   FINANCIAL REPORTING

Definition

Collection, analysis, summarisation and presentation of financial performance of a business.

2.1   Meaning

✓   Classification and recording $\Rightarrow$ *Bookkeeping*.

✓   Preparation of financial statements $\Rightarrow$ *Accounting*.

✓   Presentation and disclosure in accordance with a financial reporting framework $\Rightarrow$ *Reporting*.

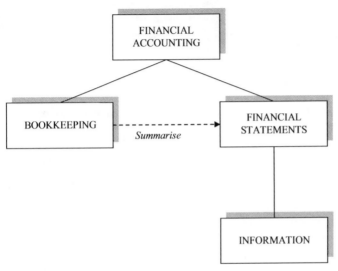

2.2 Bookkeeping

✓ "Systematic recording of financial transactions of a business".

✓ Purpose – to record every financial transaction.

✓ Activities:

➢ Collecting/recording of transactions (daily)
➢ Collating/summarizing/balancing (e.g. monthly)
➢ Making year-end adjustments.

3 FINANCIAL STATEMENTS

3.1 Components

✓ Statement of financial position ("SoFP").

✓ Statement of profit or loss and other comprehensive income ("statement of comprehensive income" – SoCI):

➢ statement of profit or loss ("income statement");
➢ other comprehensive income (e.g. gains and losses).

✓ Statement of changes in equity ("SoCIE").

✓ Statement of cash flows ("CFS").

✓ Accounting policies and explanatory notes.

Non-financial statements

✓ May be included in annual report (e.g. Chairman's/ directors' statements, environmental reports, etc).

3.2 Purpose

✓ To provide *information* about:

  ➢ Financial position (e.g. solvency) $\Rightarrow SoFP$
  ➢ Financial performance (e.g. profitability) $\Rightarrow SoCI$
  ➢ Cash flows $\Rightarrow CFS$

✓ To show results of management's stewardship ("accountability").

3.3 Inter-relationship

| OPENING SOFP | + | SOCI | + | CHANGES IN EQUITY | = | CLOSING SOFP |

4 USERS

4.1 Types

✓ *Internal* (e.g. owners, employees).

✓ *External* (e.g. potential investors, banks, government).

4.2 Information needs

✓ Shareholders	✓ For decision-making ✓ To assess dividends
✓ Management	✓ To plan and control operations ✓ To make financial analysis
✓ Employees	✓ Stability and profitability ✓ Remuneration, pension ✓ For collective bargaining
✓ Prospective investors	✓ To assess risks and returns
✓ Financial institutions	✓ Providing loan facilities ✓ Repayments scheduling
✓ Suppliers	✓ Ability to pay on time ✓ Security (assets)
✓ Customers	✓ Continuity of supply
✓ Government	✓ Taxation regulation ✓ National statistics
✓ Public and media	✓ Contribution to local economy ✓ Recent developments.

1 STATEMENT OF FINANCIAL POSITION

Definition

Reports assets, liabilities and equity at a date.

1.1 Description

✓ A statement of carrying amounts ("book" values).

✓ Vertical format.

✓ All items have monetary value.

1.2 Presentation

✓ Assets/liabilities grouped in classifications.

✓ Minimum requirements for IFRS (e.g. for companies) are set out in IAS 1 (*Session 19*).

1.3 Proforma – Sole trader

Statement of Financial Position as at …			
ASSETS	$	$	$
Non-current assets	*Cost*	*Depreciation*	
Intangible assets	x	x	x
Property, plant and equipment	x	x	x
	x	x	x
Current assets			
Inventories		x	
Trade and other receivables		x	
Prepayments		x	
Cash		x	
			x
Total assets			x
CAPITAL AND LIABILITIES			
Capital and reserves			
Capital b/fwd		x	
Profit/(loss)		x	
Drawings		(x)	
Capital c/fwd			x
Non-current liabilities			
Long-term borrowings			x
Current liabilities			
Trade and other payables		x	
Accrued expenses		x	
Operating overdrafts		x	
			x
Total capital and liabilities			x

2   ASSETS

Definition

Economic resource **controlled** … has future economic benefit … is result of past financial transaction.

2.1   Non-current

- ✓ Tangible (physical).
- ✓ Intangible (without physical substance).
- ✓ Initially recorded at "cost".
- ✓ Wearing out (depreciation/amortisation).

Investments

- ✓ Usually shares in/loans to other entities.
- ✓ May be non-current or current.
- ✓ "Listed" means quoted on a recognised stock exchange.

2.2   Current

- ✓ For conversion into cash in ordinary course of business.
- ✓ Expect to hold < 1 year.

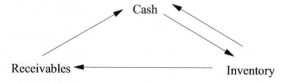

- ✓ Presented in increasing liquidity order: inventory, receivable, cash.

Inventory

- ✓ Goods for resale/ Raw materials/WIP.
- ✓ Measured at **lower** of:
  - ➢ Cost (i.e. purchase price/manufacturing cost); and
  - ➢ Net realisable value (estimated selling price – further costs).

Receivables

- ✓ Owe the entity money.
- ✓ Carrying amount is net of allowance for non-recoverability.

Prepayments

- ✓ Amounts paid on or/before end of reporting period relating to a later period.

Cash

- ✓ Cheques, bank notes, coins and "demand" deposits.
- ✓ "Petty" cash.

2.3   Net assets

- ✓ Total assets – Total liabilities = Capital and reserves (shareholders' "funds")

3   LIABILITIES

Definition

Financial obligation (or cash required to satisfy contractual terms of such an obligation).

Implies legal responsibilities to other parties:

✓   *External* (e.g. suppliers and employees).

Non-current

✓   Loans (usually interest-bearing).

✓   Provisions falling due > 1 year.

✓   Others (e.g. pension liabilities, deferred tax) are *ex-syllabus*.

Current

✓   Amounts owed due for payment < 1 year after year end:

➢   trade payables (to suppliers);

➢   "overdrawn" bank account.

Accrued expenses

✓   Amounts invoiced after the year end for goods/services provided before the year end.

✓   The "opposite" of prepayments.

4   STATEMENT OF COMPREHENSIVE INCOME

4.1   Presentation

✓   Either:

➢   *Single* statement of comprehensive income; or

➢   *Two* statements:

(1)   profit or loss; and
(2)   other comprehensive income.

4.2   Profit or loss

✓   Summarises financial operations for a specific period of time:

➢   Trading account
(Revenue – cost of sales = Gross profit)

➢   Profit and loss ("income and expenditure") account (all other items of income and expenditure).

✓   Shows profit or loss for period *before* other comprehensive income.

4.3   Other comprehensive income

✓   Other items of income and expense not recognised in profit or loss!

✓   Only a surplus arising on revaluation of a property is examinable in F3.

4.4 Proforma – Sole trader

✓ Note, for *manufacturing* entity cost of goods sold = manufacturing cost:

> Raw materials + production labour + overheads

```
         STATEMENT OF PROFIT OR LOSS
           FOR THE YEAR ENDED …
                                    $        $
Revenue                                      x
Less:   Cost of sales
        Opening inventory          x
        Add: Purchases             x
        Less: Closing inventory   (x)
                                  ___
= Cost of goods sold                        (x)
                                            ___
Gross profit                                 x

Other operating income                       x
Less: Expenses
        Distribution costs         x
        Administrative expenses    x
                                  ___
                                            (x)
                                            ___
Profit for the year                          x
                                            ___
```

4.5 Trading account

✓ Profit measures:

> ➤ Gross profit – calculated in *Trading account*
> ➤ Profit or loss ("net income") – calculated in *Profit and loss account.*

✓ Gross profit *margin*: $\dfrac{\text{Gross profit}}{\text{Revenue}} \times 100$

Revenue

✓ Reflects *all* sales made to customers.

✓ A sale is usually recognised when goods despatched/services rendered.

✓ Sales made but not paid for = Trade receivables.

Cost of sales

✓ Cost of goods actually sold = all costs associated with purchase/manufacture.

✓ Costs are "matched" with revenues earned.

Closing inventory

✓ Inventory held at the end of a trading period.
✓ Counted and valued (normally at cost).
✓ Deducted from cost of sales/included in inventory (an asset) – will be expense next year.

✓

1 ACCOUNTING SYSTEMS

Records and procedures, formal and informal, relating to the assembling, recording, retrieval and reporting of financial information that also provide necessary *internal controls*. 1.1 Qualities of useful information

- ✓ Relevant
- ✓ Complete
- ✓ Objective
- ✓ Cost effective
- ✓ Concise
- ✓ Reliable
- ✓ Accurate
- ✓ Comparable
- ✓ User-friendly
- ✓ Timely

1.2 Organisational objectives

- ✓ Orderly and efficient business conduct.
- ✓ Adherence to management policies.
- ✓ Safeguarding of assets.
- ✓ Prevention/detection of fraud/error.
- ✓ Accuracy and completeness of accounting records.
- ✓ Timely preparation of reliable financial information.

Internal controls ensure

- ✓ Transactions are authorised (i.e. valid).
- ✓ All transactions and other events are recorded promptly, accurately and completely.
- ✓ Access to assets and records is restricted.
- ✓ Recorded assets exist.

1.3 Accounting records

All records of monetary transactions, assets and liabilities (includes books of prime entry, ledgers, documentation).

2 SALES

2.1 Documentation

- ✓ Customer order (oral/written).
- ✓ Quotation for bulk discounts, customised products.

In "standard form"

- ✓ Sales order (SO) – customer, product(s), quantities ± prices.

- ✓ Goods despatch note (GDN) – SO + delivery details.

- ✓ Sales invoice – GDN details + prices + tax.

- ✓ Customer statement (extracted from receivables ledger).

2.2 Recording

- ✓ Sales invoice in SDB

- ✓ D/E from **SDB**

Dr	Trade receivables	$x	
	Cr Revenue		$x

✓ Credit notes to customer (in **SDB** or returns book)

Dr	Revenue	$x	
	Cr Trade receivables		$x

2.3 Reconciliation

✓ List of receivables ledger balances to control a/c

3 PURCHASES/EXPENSES

3.1 Documentation

In "standard written form"

✓ Purchase requisition.

✓ Purchase order (PO) – supplier, product(s), quantities (may be + prices also).

✓ Goods/services received note (GRN) – PO details + delivery details.

Received from supplier

✓ Purchase invoice – product(s), quantities, prices + tax.

✓ Credit note (e.g. for goods returns).

✓ Supplier's statement (extracted from supplier's receivables ledger).

3.2 Recording

✓ Purchase invoice in PDB

✓ D/E from **PDB**

Dr	Purchases/expenses	$x	
	Cr Trade payables		$x

✓ Credit note in PDB (or purchases returns)

Dr	Trade receivables	$x	
	Cr Purchases/expenses		$x

3.3 Reconciliations

✓ Individual payables ledger balances to supplier's statement.

✓ List of payables ledger balances to control a/c.

4 CASH

4.1 Documentation

Receipts

✓ Remittance advice (accompanying receipt from customer).

✓ Cash (cheque, bank order/transfer).

Payments

- ✓ Payment requisition.
- ✓ Cash (cheque, bank order/transfer).

4.2 Recording

- ✓ Cash in cash book.
- ✓ D/E from cash book.

Receipts

Dr	Cash	$x	
	Cr Receivables		$x

Payments

Dr	Payables	$x	
	Cr Cash		$x

4.3 Reconciliation

- ✓ Cash book balance to bank statement.

5 INVENTORY

5.1 Documentation

Received

- ✓ Advice/delivery note (from supplier).
- ✓ Goods received note (GRN).

Despatched

- ✓ Goods despatch note (GRN).

5.2 Recording

- ✓ On "bin card" or other inventory records.

5.3 Reconciliation

- ✓ Quantities on inventory records to physical balances.

6 TANGIBLE NON-CURRENT ASSETS

6.1 Documentation

Purchase

- ✓ Capital expenditure requisition.
- ✓ Other as for purchases.

Disposal

- ✓ Authority to dispose (scrap/sell/part-exchange).
- ✓ Sales invoice.

6.2 Recording

- ✓ Purchase/sales invoice in PDB/SDB.
- ✓ Cash paid/received in cash book.
- ✓ Asset register.

6.3 Reconciliation

- ✓ Items in asset register to physical assets.

1 BUSINESS ENTITY CONCEPT

Definition

Accounting applies to a business entity that is separate and distinct from its owner(s).

- ✓ Business entity may be *legally* separated from owners.
- ✓ If not legally distinguishable must be distinct from owners for *accounting purposes*.
- ✓ Transactions between an entity and its owners are *separately identified* and accounted for from *entity's perspective*.

2 DUALITY

Every transaction has a dual effect.

- ✓ Second effect is equal to and "opposite" to the first.
- ✓ All effects are considered from **entity's perspective**.

3 ACCOUNTING EQUATION

3.1 The principle

- ✓ At any point in time:

Net assets (i.e. Assets – Liabilities) = Equity

- ✓ Consequently, a change in net assets *must* equal change in equity in any period:

Closing net assets	–	Opening net assets	=	Capital introduced in period	+	Profit – Loss	–	Appropriations (e.g. distributions)

3.2 Equity

Residual interest in assets after deducting all liabilities.

A "Framework" definition

Components

- ✓ Capital: investment by the owner(s);
- ✓ Retained earnings ("accumulated profits"): profits less losses earned and retained.
- ✓ Appropriations to owners:
  - ➢ "drawings" by sole traders (money/goods);
  - ➢ salaries and profit shares (to partners);
  - ➢ distributions ("dividends") to shareholders.

3.3 The equation

- ✓ Underlies presentation of statement of financial position (also called "balance sheet"):

Assets = Equity + Liabilities

STAGES

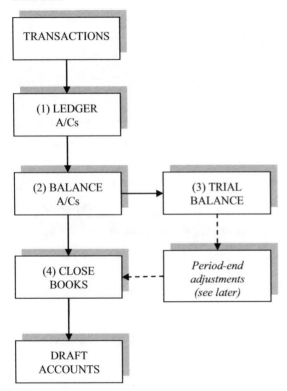

1 LEDGER ACCOUNTS

1.1 Double entry bookkeeping

- ✓ Based on concept of "dual effect".
- ✓ Every debit has a matching credit (and vice versa).
- ✓ One account for each type of transaction.
- ✓ Depicted as "T" accounts.

Convention

- ✓ Dr (left)   Cr (right)

"Balance sheet" * a/c

Dr entry represents		Cr entry represents	
1 ASSET	↑ or	1 LIABILITY	↑ or
2 LIABILITY	↓	2 ASSET	↓

* Remember this is common name for SoFP.

I&E a/c

Dr entry represents		Cr entry represents	
1 EXPENSE	↑ or	1 INCOME	↑ or
2 INCOME	↓	2 EXPENSE	↓

2 BALANCING ACCOUNTS

2.1 Purpose

✓ Helps ensure D/E recorded correctly.

✓ Means to "strike (i.e. arrive at) a balance".

✓ Balancing amounts inserted are:

  ➢ Carried down ("c/d") or forward ("c/f")
  ➢ Brought down ("b/d") or forward ("b/f").

✓ Can be done *at any time.*

✓ *Always* done before books are "closed".

2.2 Procedure

(1) Cast (i.e. sum) Dr side and note total.
  Cast Cr side and note total.

(2) Write the *larger* amount as total on both sides.

(3) Insert balancing figure ("c/fwd") so both sides are equal

  (a) $\Sigma Drs > \Sigma Crs \Rightarrow$ Dr balance
              b/fwd on Dr side of a/c.

  (b) $\Sigma Crs > \Sigma Drs \Rightarrow$ Cr balance
              b/fwd on Cr side of a/c

3 TRIAL BALANCE

3.1 Extracting a list of balances

✓ Simply a list of *all* Dr and all Cr balances on individual ledger a/cs.

✓ Links ledger a/cs $\Rightarrow$ financial statements.

✓ Balances can be *extracted* (i.e. listed) at any time.

✓ *Always* done as at the end of a reporting period.

4 CLOSING THE BOOKS

4.1 Two types of account

✓ Income and expense a/cs – these are "closed off" (totals transferred to profit and loss a/c).

✓ Asset and liability a/cs – closing balances are simply b/d as opening balances (in next accounting period).

5 DRAFTING ACCOUNTS

✓ The process of presenting transactions and balances in prescribed formats.

1 CREDIT TRANSACTIONS

1.1 Credit sale

✓ On sale:

D/E	Dr	Trade receivable	
	Cr		Sales

✓ On receipt of cash:

D/E	Dr	Cash	
	Cr		Trade receivable

1.2 Credit purchase

✓ On purchase:

D/E	Dr	Purchases	
	Cr		Trade payable

✓ On payment of cash:

D/E	Dr	Trade payable	
	Cr		Cash

2 DISCOUNTS

2.1 Trade

✓ Price reductions to trade customers (cash or credit) is *unconditional*.

✓ Original sale/purchase is recorded at **net** amount (**after** discount). So discount is **not** separately recorded.

✓ Also called "bulk" and "volume" discounts.

2.2 Settlement

✓ Apply ONLY to transactions on credit terms.

✓ *Conditional* on prompt/early payment (settlement).

✓ Original sale is recorded at:

> **net** amount, if discount is expected to be taken;
> **gross** amount, if not expected to be taken.

✓ Purchase it always recorded **gross** and discount recorded separately, if taken.

Settlement discount on sales

✓ Sale is recorded net or gross depending on whether customer is expected to take advantage of discount.

✓ If settlement is contrary to expectation, discount is an adjustment against **revenue**.

✓ For example, customer takes discount when sale is recorded gross:

D/E	Dr	Revenue a/c	$x	
	Cr	Trade receivable		$x

Received – from suppliers

✓ Purchase is always recorded gross, therefore …

✓ Discount decreases payable and expense:

D/E	Dr	Trade payables a/c	$x	
	Cr	Discounts received a/c	$x	

✓ Statement of profit or loss may include:

> ➤ gross purchases and discounts allowed *separately*;
> ➤ *net* purchases (i.e. net of discounts).

3 RETURNS

3.1 Sales (Returns in)

✓ On issue of credit note:

D/E	Dr	Sales returns (or Revenue)
	Cr	Trade receivables

Reduce amount to be received.

✓ If cash refunded:

D/E	Dr	Trade receivables
	Cr	Cash

A cash refund.

3.2 Purchases (Returns out)

✓ On receipt of credit note:

D/E	Dr	Trade payables
	Cr	Purchase returns (or Purchases)

✓ If cash refunded:

D/E	Dr	Cash
	Cr	Trade payables

1 ROLE

1.1 Nature

✓ List of all Dr and all Cr balances on individual ledger accounts.

✓ Expect balances to be:

➢ Dr – asset and expense a/cs
➢ Cr – liability and income a/cs.

✓ No prescribed order. Examples:

➢ alphabetically by name;
➢ order of appearance in financial statements.

1.2 Purposes

(1) To assist in detection of *bookkeeping* errors.

(2) To prepare *accounts* via extended trial balance (ETB).

Questions answered

? Is D/E correct in principle? (i.e. every Dr has equivalent Cr?)

? Has every ledger account been correctly cast?

? Have balances been correctly calculated and recorded in the correct Dr/Cr column?

? Have Dr and Cr columns of TB been added up correctly?

Advantages

✓ Agreed TB provides *prima facie* evidence of arithmetic accuracy of "books of account".

✓ Errors revealed can be corrected before financial statements are drafted.

Limitations

✗ Does **not** prove *accuracy* of allocation/classification and recording.

✗ Does **not** prove *completeness* (i.e. no omissions).

2 ERROR DETECTION

2.1 Types of error

Identified

Because $\sum Drs \neq \sum Crs$.

- ✓ Single-sided, unequal and double-sided entries.

- ✓ Casting errors in ledger a/cs.

- ✓ Balances b/fwd on "wrong side" of ledger a/cs.

- ✓ Ledger a/c balances omitted when extracting.

- ✓ Transposition errors ($\div 9$).

Errors not identified

- ✗ Original (prime) entry – initial recording at wrong amount.

- ✗ Omission – transaction not recorded.

- ✗ Commission ("carelessness") – misclassification (but not "in principle").

- ✗ Principle – revenue items as capital (or *vice versa*).

- ✗ Compensating – neutralisation by equivalent opposite error(s).

3 FINANCIAL STATEMENTS PREPARATION

3.1 Extended Trial Balance (ETB)

- ✓ TB can be extracted *any time.*

- ✓ Financial accounts prepared at *period end* via ETB.

- ✓ ETB is a "work sheet" which makes adjustments:
  - ➢ to correct errors identified by TB
  - ➢ to account for period-end adjustments.

Period-end adjustments

- ✓ Accruals and prepayments.
- ✓ Depreciation.
- ✓ Allowance for irrecoverable debts.
- ✓ Inventory.

1 ACCRUAL BASIS

1.1 Accruals concept

Revenue and costs

- ✓ Recognised as *earned or incurred* **not** when cash is received/paid.

- ✓ Recorded in periods to which they relate.

- ✓ Assumption about *timing*.

1.2 Consequences

Expenses

- ✓ Paid in advance ⇒ *Prepaid* expense ("Prepayment")

- ✓ Incurred but not paid ⇒ Accrued *expense*

Income

- ✓ Received in advance ⇒ *Deferred* income

- ✓ Earned but not paid ⇒ Accrued *income*

"Matching concept"

- ✓ Expenses should be matched against revenue *generated*.

Prudence concept

- ✓ *Future* income **cannot** be recognised.

2 EXPENSES

2.1 Traditional approach

- ✓ Use **only ONE "T" a/c.**
- ✓ Calculate accrued expense/prepayment.
- ✓ C/fwd accrual/prepayment (liability/asset on expense a/c)
- ✓ Expense is balancing figure on "T" a/c.
- ✓ *Alternatively calculate expense ⇒ c/fwd is balancing figure – but above is usually easier.*

Advantages

- ✓ No need to maintain separate accrual/prepayment accounts for balances.

- ✓ Simpler (especially in manual systems).

2.2 Alternative/"reversal" approach

- ✓ Use **TWO "T"** a/cs.

- ✓ Calculate accrual/prepayment.

- ✓ If prepaid:

D/E	**Dr**	**Prepayments a/c**
	Cr	Expense a/c

- ✓ If accrual:

D/E	Dr	Expense a/c
	Cr	**Accrued expense a/c**

✓ "Reverse" these *period-end adjustments* at beginning of new accounting period.

2.3 Practicalities

✓ A prepayment can be calculated (as the advance payment is known amount).

✓ An accrual is usually an accounting estimate.

✓ Any difference between estimate and actual is Dr/Cr to profit or loss in the following year's expense.

Exam Tip: It is unnecessary to "prove" charge to profit or loss with a calculation.

3 INCOME

3.1 Traditional approach

✓ As for expenses but calculate *accrued/deferred income*.

3.2 Alternative/"reversal" approach

✓ As for expenses but:

✓ If accrued ("opposite" of accrued expense treatment):

D/E **Dr Accrued income a/c**
　　　 Cr　　Income a/c

✓ If deferred ("opposite" of prepaid expense):

D/E Dr Income a/c
　　　 Cr Deferred income a/c

4 SUMMARY OF ACCOUNTING EFFECTS

4.1 Expenses

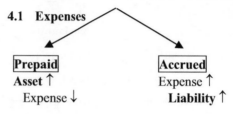

4.2 Income

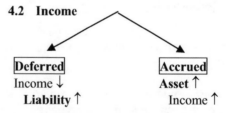

(Deferred income is a liability if there is an obligation to repay.)

1 NON-CURRENT ASSETS

Definition

Assets expected to be used during more than one accounting period ...

1.1 Tangible

✓ Monetary assets with physical substance:

> ➤ Property, plant and equipment;
> ➤ Investments (excluding short-term).

1.2 Intangible assets (see section 23)

✓ Non-monetary assets without physical substance:

> ➤ Rights (e.g. copyrights, patented rights)
> ➤ Manufacturing licences
> ➤ Goodwill
> ➤ Development costs
> ➤ Brands.

1.3 IAS 16 (see detail in section 22)

Principal issues

✓ Asset recognition.
✓ Determination of carrying amount.
✓ Recognition of depreciation.

2 DEPRECIATION

2.1 Concept

✓ Only revenue expenditure (**not** capital expenditure) is charged to profit or loss.

✓ Apart from *land,* assets wear out (time and use).

✓ Capital costs are "spread" and expensed over *useful lives* ("matching concept").

2.2 Definitions (simplified)

Property, plant and equipment – Tangible assets held for use in production/supply of goods/services (or for admin) and expected to be used during > 12 months.

Depreciation – Systematic allocation of *depreciable amount* over useful life.

Depreciable amount – Cost (or revalued amount) less *residual value*.

Useful life – Period over which asset is expected to be used.

Cost – Amount of cash paid to acquire/construct.

Residual value – Net amount expected to be obtained at end of useful life less expected disposal costs.

Carrying amount – Amount recognised in SoFP (after deducting accumulated depreciation).

2.3 Methods

✓ Generally based on:

  ➢ Passage of time (e.g. straight-line, reducing balance); or
  ➢ Level of activity (e.g. units of production).

Straight line

✓ Recognises "consumption" of benefits (through use) on pro-rata basis.

✓ Is "default basis" (i.e. if no pattern of consumption).

✓ Formula: $\dfrac{\text{Cost - Residual value *}}{\text{Useful life *}}$

* Accounting estimates.

✓ Expressed as:

  ➢ "straight line over n years"; or
  ➢ x% per year on cost.

Reducing balance ("reducing instalment")

✓ $\Rightarrow$ Progressively decreasing expense over useful life.
✓ Used where consumption is highest initially.
✓ Residual value generally ignored.
✓ Formula:

  Carrying amount × annual depreciation rate (%)

Advantages

Straight-line	**Reducing balance**
✓ Simple – "one-off" annual calculation	✓ "Accelerated" expense reflects greater use in earlier years
✓ Constant expense (does not distort)	✓ Assets in use never fully depreciated.
✓ Easy to calculate accumulated depreciation (e.g. annual charge × n years).	✓ No need to separately identify assets (until disposal).

Disadvantages

Straight-line	**Reducing balance**
✗ Unrealistic ($\neq$ consumption of benefits)	✗ Calculations more complex.
✗ No expense after useful life (assets still in use).	

2.4 Ledger accounting

Asset cost a/c

- ✓ As long as asset is owned this shows original purchase price (or cost of construction).

- ✓ Exception is revaluation (see section 22).

Depreciation

- ✓ Expense (charge) for year $\Rightarrow$ Dr.

- ✓ Reduction in carrying amount $\Rightarrow$ Cr.

- ✓ Entries:

Dr	Depreciation expense a/c	$x
	Cr Accumulated depreciation a/c	$x

- ✓ At end of reporting period:

Dr	Profit or loss a/c	$x
	Cr Depreciation expense a/c	$x

Accumulated depreciation

- ✓ Balance c/fwd and b/fwd at end of each year is increased by charge for year.

- ✓ But see **disposals** (later).

2.5 Changes in estimates

- ✓ Are **not** errors.
- ✓ Change is reflected in depreciation expense of current and future periods.

Useful life

- ✓ Depreciation is calculated on remaining life.

- ✓ Formula (straight line): $\dfrac{\text{Depreciable amount}}{\text{Remaining useful life}}$

Residual value

- ✓ Most likely to apply to straight line method.
- ✓ A reduction in estimate (most likely) simply increases depreciable amount.

3 DISPOSALS

3.1 Ledger accounting

- ✓ Transfer cost and accumulated depreciation to disposals:

  D/E

Dr	Disposals a/c	$Cost
	Cr Asset a/c	$Cost

Dr	Accumulated depreciation a/c	$Acc^d dep^n
	Cr Disposals a/c	$Acc^d dep^n

✓ Account for proceeds:

D/E

Dr   Cash (or receivable) a/c $x
    Cr   Disposals a/c $x

✓ At end of year – transfer profit or loss on disposal (i.e. balance on disposals a/c) to profit or loss (P or L).

➢ Profit on sale (= over depreciation):

D/E

Dr   Disposals a/c   Cr   P or L a/c

➢ Loss on sale (= under depreciation)

D/E

Dr   P or L a/c   Cr   Disposals a/c

3.2 Part exchange/ "trade-in"

Trade-in allowance ($x)

= Part of cost of new   = Proceeds on sale of
        asset   old asset

Dr Asset cost a/c   Cr Disposals a/c

✓ In summary:

Dr   Asset a/c $(x + y)
    Cr   Cash (or bank) a/c $y
    Cr   Disposals a/c $x

4   REVALUATION

4.1   Appreciating assets

Revaluation of an asset (e.g. property) does **not** eliminate requirement for depreciation ... **except** land.

✓ Carrying amount = revaluation amount – subsequent accumulated depreciation.

✓ Gain is *unrealised* (i.e. **not** recognised in profit or loss).

D/E

		$	$
Dr	Asset	x	
Cr	Other comprehensive income		x

✓ Gains are accumulated in a revaluation surplus in SoCIE (see *section 19*).

5 PRACTICAL POINTS

5.1 Depreciation calculations

✓ Apply same method *consistently* to **all** similar assets.

✓ Usually from date brought into use (may be legal requirement).

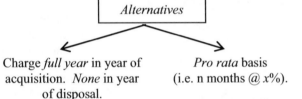

Charge *full year* in year of acquisition. *None* in year of disposal.

Pro rata basis (i.e. n months @ x%).

Exam Tip! If purchase date not specified ⇒ NO choice but to charge full year. Always READ THE QUESTION.

5.2 Ledger accounts

✓ Use one for each category of asset (with same depreciation policy).

Advantage

✓ Assuming no residual values, calculate annual depreciation on year-end balance (after accounting for all additions and disposals).

Disadvantage

✘ If using straight line method, take care not to charge depreciation on already fully-depreciated assets.

5.3 Short-cut calculations

✓ Assuming a full year's charge in the year of purchase and none in the year of sale.

Straight line method

✓ Adjust **cost** for additions/disposals and calculate depreciation on **cost**.

Reducing balance method

✓ Adjust cost **and accumulated depreciation** for additions/disposals and calculate depreciation on **carrying amount**.

5.4 Fixed asset register

✓ Simply a log of all tangible non-current assets.

✓ Uses:

➢ calculating depreciation
➢ identifying fully-depreciated assets
➢ historic information to account for disposals
➢ in periodic physical inspection (to ensure existence).

0905

1 TRADE ACCOUNTS

Definitions

Receivables – Amount *due* … to satisfy a debt or a claim.
Payables – Amounts *owed* … but not yet paid.

1.1 Examples

Receivables	*Payables*
✓ Trade receivables	✓ Trade payables
✓ Rents due (from tenants)	✓ Rents owed (to landlord)
✓ Loan and interest receivables	✓ Loans and interest payables (including penalties)
✓ Advance payments (to suppliers)	✓ Advance payments (from customers)
✓ Amounts due from group companies	✓ Unpaid dividends ("declared")
✓ Tax refunds.	✓ Amounts due to group companies
	✓ Unpaid salaries and wages
	✓ Tax liabilities (e.g. sales tax, payroll taxes)

1.2 Credit facilities

Types

✓ Loans and overdraft facilities.

✓ Leases.

✓ Hire purchase.

✓ "Buy now, pay later" schemes.

✓ Credit cards.

Advantages

✓ Immediate use of purchased item.

✓ Minimises risk (of theft) of physical cash.

✓ Items otherwise not affordable.

✓ Convenience (e.g. on-line shopping).

Disadvantages

✗ More expensive (interest/penalties).

✗ Additional costs (e.g. handling fees).

✗ Risk of "living beyond means".

✗ Administrative costs and risk of irrecoverable debts.

✗ May require security/other guarantee.

2 RECEIVABLES

2.1 Accounting entries

✓ Sale:

D/E	Dr	Trade receivable a/c	$x	
	Cr	Revenue a/c		$x

✓ Cash received:

D/E	Dr	Cash a/c	$x	
	Cr	Trade receivable a/c		$x

Aged receivable ("debt") analysis

✓ To know how long owed.
✓ Analysis by when due.
✓ Facilitates sending reminders/final notices.

2.2 Indicators of irrecoverable debts

✓ Taking longer to pay than usual.
✓ Payments by instalments (not on agreed terms).
✓ Regular disputing of invoices (delaying tactic).
✓ Receivership (administration)/liquidation.

2.3 Credit limits

A threshold … the maximum amount risked "on account".

Purpose

✓ To limit exposure to risk of non-payment.

Benefits

✓ Frees up time for other tasks.
✓ Speeds up sales process.
✓ Improves collection.
✓ An account monitoring tool.

3 IRRECOVERABLE DEBTS

"Bad" debts: Uncollectible/unrecoverable debts.
"Write-off": Removing asset (debt) and charging to profit or loss.

3.1 Double entry

D/E	Dr	"Bad" debt expense* a/c	$x	
	Cr	Trade receivable a/c		$x

* NOT to Revenue a/c

3.2 Loss allowance

✓ Recognises that not all debtors will pay in full.

✓ Expected credit loss is recognised (as expense) when risk of non-recovery is first identified.

✓ Carrying amount (in SOFP) is **net** of loss allowance.

✓ Record of **gross** amount due is **kept** in books.

✓ To allow is **not** the same as to write off.

✓ Is **not** the same as a provision (i.e. **not** a liability).

3.3 Accounting entries

✓ Any initial allowance is adjusted at the end of each subsequent reporting period.

✓ Any difference between opening and closing allowances is charge (if increase) or credit (if decrease) to profit or loss.

✓ D/E works out expense.

Allowance for irrecoverable debts a/c

	$		$
		Opening bal b/d	x
Bad debt expense		Bad debt expense	
(= decrease)	x	(= increase)	x
Closing bal c/d	x		
	x		x
		Opening bal b/d	x

Bad debt expense a/c

	$		$
Allowance		Allowances	
(increase)	x	(decrease)	x

3.4 Calculating components

Specific

- ✓ Made against amounts due from specific customers.
- ✓ Against whole or partial amounts.
- ✓ Account receivable is kept intact (gross amount).

General

- ✓ Further allowance.

- ✓ Against **other** balances (i.e. no specific allowance made).

- ✓ Usually a %.

Total charge to profit or loss

Write-offs of irrecoverable amounts
+ Increase in Specific/General allowance
– Decrease in Specific/General allowance
– Any write back ("recovery")

3.5 When "doubtful" debts go "bad"

- ✓ Now "write-off" account (i.e. remove from books).

- ✓ Do **not** "match" against any allowance already made.

- ✓ Allowances no longer required will be "automatically" taken care of.

3.6 Summary

(1) Write-off bad debts:

Dr	Irrecoverable debt expense a/c	$x	
	Cr Trade receivable a/c		$x

(2) Calculate allowances (balance to carry down).

(3) Charge/(credit) change in allowances to expense a/c.

(4) Total expense = (1) ± (3)

4 SUBSEQUENT RECOVERY

4.1 Of a doubtful debt

- ✓ Normal D/E applies (as account is still "on the books"):

Dr	Cash a/c
	Cr Trade receivable a/c

- ✓ Allowance no longer required is *automatically credited* to expense a/c (and profit or loss).

4.2 Of a debt written off

If recognised

- ✓ Since there is no account "on the books":

D/E	Dr	Cash a/c (Asset)
	Cr	Irrecoverable debt expense* a/c

* Or "Sundry income" a/c

If not recognised

✓ Cash receipt as usual:

D/E	Dr	Cash a/c (Asset)
	Cr	Trade receivable a/c (Asset) ←

✓ THEN reverse credit balance*:

D/E	Dr	Trade receivable a/c (Asset) ←
	Cr	Irrecoverable debt a/c

"Cancel out"

* If receipt is less than amount previously written off the whole amount should be reinstated if full recovery is now expected.

5   TRADE PAYABLES

5.1   Settlement

✓ Usually cash/bank transfer, etc.

✓ May be reduced by settlement discounts.

✓ "Contra" entry – agreed offset against amount owed to same supplier (**lower** amount).

5.2   Supplier statements

Timing differences	Supplier's statement	Buyer's books
Purchase invoices (raised by supplier)	Included	Excluded (e.g. goods not yet received and/or invoice not processed)
Credit notes (raised by supplier)	Included	Excluded (e.g. not yet processed)
Debit notes (raised by customer)	Excluded (e.g. returned goods not yet received)	Included (pending receipt of credit note from supplier)
Cash payments	Excluded (e.g. not yet received)	Included

Errors – examples

✓ Charging goods/services to wrong customer.
✓ Recording wrong amounts.
✓ Omissions.

Reconciliations

✓ Are performed periodically.
✓ Timing differences are reconciling items.
  Adjustments (accounting entries) made only for errors.

1 INVENTORY

1.1 Categories

- ✓ Goods purchased for resale.
- ✓ Consumable stores.
- ✓ Raw materials and components (for production).
- ✓ Work in progress.
- ✓ Finished goods.

1.2 Inventory records

- ✓ May be a legal requirement.

Methods

- ✓ Continuous – show all movements and balances.
- ✓ Period-end – physical count ("stock take").

Stock checking of continuous records

- ✓ Control system includes:

  - ➤ scheduled test-counting (all items at least once a year);

  - ➤ investigation and correction of count differences.

1.3 Measurement (IAS 2 "Inventories")

- ✓ **Lower** of cost and net realisable value (NRV).

2 ACCOUNTING ENTRIES

2.1 Closing inventory

- ✓ In SoFP *(an asset)*
- ✓ In profit or loss (reduces cost of goods sold).

D/E	Dr	Inventory a/c	$x	
	Cr	Trading a/c (closing inventory)		$x

2.2 Opening inventory

- ✓ Opening inventory $\Rightarrow$ cost of goods sold (i.e. expense).

D/E	Dr	Trading a/c	$x	
	Cr	Inventory a/c (opening inventory)		$x

1 BOOKS OF PRIME ENTRY

1.1 Overview

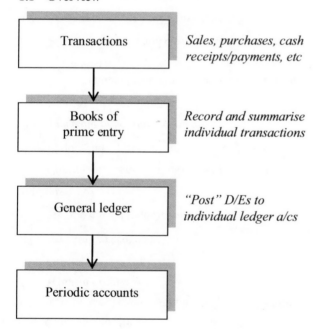

Transactions — *Sales, purchases, cash receipts/payments, etc*

Books of prime entry — *Record and summarise individual transactions*

General ledger — *"Post" D/Es to individual ledger a/cs*

Periodic accounts

1.2 "Day books"

✓ Simply lists – not part of D/E system:

> ➤ *Sales* day book (SDB)
> ➤ *Sales returns* day book
> ➤ *Purchases* day book (PDB)
> ➤ *Purchase returns* day book
> ➤ *Cash* book
> ➤ *Petty cash* book
> ➤ *Journal.*

1.3 Ledgers

✓ General (nominal) – records all double-entries.

Other

✓ Sales (receivables) – individual customers' personal a/cs.

✓ Purchases (payables) – individual suppliers' personal a/cs.

Maintaining D/E

✓ If a separate ledger records transactions "outside" general ledger, general ledger must **include** a control account for that ledger (for totals).

✓ If a sub-ledger is **included** in general ledger ("integrated"), a control account is maintained "outside" the general ledger (for control purposes).

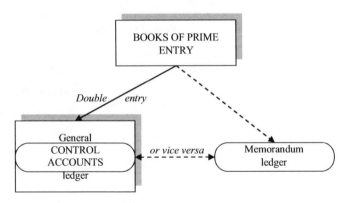

2 SALES DAY BOOK

2.1 Posting to general ledger

Posting what?	Also needed IN MEMORANDUM*
✓ Individual transactions	⇒ Totals (in a control a/c)
OR	OR
✓ Totals	⇒ Individual transactions (in a ledger)

2.2 Comparison

✓ For example, credit sales posted from SDB:

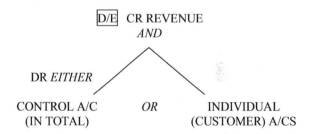

D/E CR REVENUE
AND

DR *EITHER*

CONTROL A/C   *OR*   INDIVIDUAL
(IN TOTAL)   (CUSTOMER) A/CS

3 PURCHASES DAY BOOK

3.1 Description

✓ All expenditure (capital and revenue) obtained on credit (not just purchases of goods).

✓ Therefore *analysed* by general ledger a/cs for summarisation and posting.

3.2 Posting to general ledger

✓ SAME principles as for SDB.

4 CASH BOOK

4.1 Records

✓ **Bank** account receipts and payments of:

> ➢ physical cash (notes and coins);
> ➢ cheques/money orders;
> ➢ money transfers/bank drafts, etc.

4.2 Discounts

Discounts allowed

✓ If not expected to be taken (i.e. sale recorded gross) record in separate column as a reminder.

✓ Posting, for example of totals:

Dr   Revenue $x
      Cr   Receivable ledger control a/c $x

And individual amounts recorded in individual customer's account.

✓ Same principle applies to settlement discounts received from suppliers.

5 PETTY CASH

Definition

Small fund of cash for incidental expenses (of "petty" nature).

5.1 Imprest system

✓ A *fixed* sum of money ... for petty expenditure.

✓ Every payment must be supported with a voucher.

$\Rightarrow$ Cash + Vouchers = Imprest balance

✓ Periodic reimbursement of amount of vouchers:

Dr   Petty cash a/c $x
      Cr   Bank a/c $x

✓ Cash (payments) book has petty cash column.

5.2　Non-imprest

✓　Fixed amount issued periodically or when a balance reached (may be nil).

Disadvantages

✗　Less incentive to ensure all disbursements supported/ documented.

✗　More difficult to reconcile.

5.3　Controls and security

Objective

✓　To ensure disbursements only for *valid* transactions and *accurately* recorded.

Basic controls

✓　Imprest system.

✓　Approval (authorised signature) for replenishment.

✓　Cancellation of vouchers to prevent reuse.

✓　Sequential numbering of vouchers.

✓　Limit on amount for any one payment.

6　THE JOURNAL

6.1　Purpose

To record transactions not in other day books (to ensure controlled and authorised).

✓　All adjustments must be recorded in general ledger before books can be closed.

✓　Period-end adjustments are posted to general ledger after extraction of trial balance.

Examples

✓　Non-routine transfers (e.g. "part-exchange").

✓　Period-end adjustments:

➢　depreciation;
➢　asset disposals;
➢　irrecoverable debt write-offs and allowances;
➢　inventory.

✓　Correction of errors.

6.2 Layout

✓ Dr entry is **always** written first.

Date	Narrative	A/c refs	Dr	Cr
	Being . . .		$	$

7 SALES TAX

7.1 General principles

✓ Applied to purchase and sale of goods/services on value added ("VAT").

✓ Paid to (or recovered from) government agency.

✓ Suffered by "end-user".

7.1 Operation

✓ SDB and PDB have "gross", "tax" and "net" columns.

✓ Business is a collecting agent – liable to pay excess of tax on revenue over tax on expenses.

8 CONTROL ACCOUNTS

8.1 Where kept

✓ In general ledger, if D/E uses *totals*.

OR

✓ In memorandum, if D/E use *individual transactions*.

8.2 Importance in control

> If all postings are correct $\sum$ Individual balances
> = Balance on control account.

✓ List of individual ledger balances is extracted periodically and summed.

✓ Usually done **before** extraction of trial balance.

✓ Errors in postings to general ledger would cause trial balance not to balance (unless compensating errors).

✓ Errors in individual accounts may result in wrong amounts being paid/received.

8.3 Discrepancies

✓ Any difference must be reconciled and errors corrected.

✓ May be omissions, duplications or other mis-posting (e.g. transpositions).

1 CONTROL ACCOUNTS

1.1 Maintained in general ledger

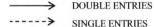

→ DOUBLE ENTRIES

- - - - -> SINGLE ENTRIES

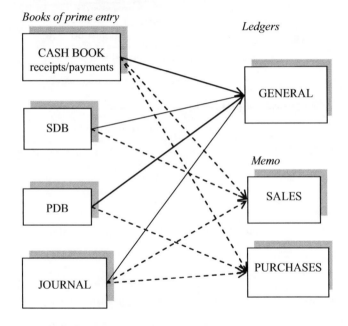

Books of prime entry

1.2 Internal control

✓ If all postings (individual and total) are correct $\Rightarrow$

$\sum$ Individual balances = Control a/c balance

✓ Errors in general ledger $\Rightarrow$ Trial balance will not balance.

✓ Errors in individual a/c $\Rightarrow$

➢ over/(under *) payments to suppliers

➢ under/(over *) receipts from customers.
* less likely to remain undetected.

✓ Reconciliations identify errors for correction.

1.3 Procedure

✓ Balance individual a/cs, extract list and sum $\Rightarrow$ A

✓ Balance control a/c $\Rightarrow$ B

✓ Investigate if A $\neq$ B

✓ If A = B error could still exist (e.g. if transaction omitted from a book of prime entry).

1.4   Errors

In control a/c

✓   Casting error in book of prime entry (affects only **total**).

✓   Casting error in balancing control a/c.

✓   Transposition of **total**.

✓   Omissions of entries recorded only in individual accounts:

> ➢   "contras"
> ➢   irrecoverable debt write-offs

In individual a/cs

✓   Casting error in balancing individual a/cs.

✓   Omission/duplicate posting of **individual** transactions.

✓   Transposition of **individual** amounts.

✓   In extracting individual balances (= list):

> ➢   omission
> ➢   recording Cr balance as Dr (or vice versa).

1.5   Agreement

Step 1   Identify reasons for differences (above).

Step 2   Adjust control a/c for errors in it.

Step 3   Adjust list of balances for individual a/c errors.

2   TRADE RECEIVABLES

2.1   Proforma (TOTALS)

Receivables ledger control a/c

	$		$
Balance b/f	x	Cash received	x
Sales (per SDB)	x	Discounts allowed	x
"Bounced" cheques	x	Sales returns	x
		Bad debts	x
		Credit notes	x
		Payables contras	x
		Balance c/f	x
	x		x
Bal b/f	x		

2.2 Reconciliation

Receivables ledger control a/c

	$		$
B/f	x		
		Adjustments	x
Adjustments	x		
		Balance c/f	x
	—		
	x		x
	—		—

Do not agree

Reconciliation Statement

Now agree

	$
Total per original listing	x
Add: Errors (e.g. omissions)	x
Less: Errors (e.g. duplications)	(x)
Balance per control a/c	x

3 TRADE PAYABLES

3.1 Proforma

Payables ledger control a/c

	$		$
		Balance b/f	x
Cash paid	x		
		Purchases (per PDB)	x
Discounts received	x		
Purchase returns	x		
Receivables contras	x		
Balance c/f	x		
	—		—
	x		x
	—		—
		Balance c/f	x

Double entries

✓ Where control a/c is in general ledger any adjustments will require D/E to be made.

✓ Exception: If error made in calculation of b/f balance.

1 RECONCILIATION

1.1 Of what?

✓ Balance per bank statement (prepared by bank) to cash book balance.

Balance	Meaning customer is:	Customer has:
Cr	A creditor	An asset
Dr = "overdrawn"	A debtor	A liability

1.2 Why?

✓ To check accuracy of cash book postings.

✓ An *independent check* (internal control).

1.3 Reasons for differences

(1) Bank lacks knowledge of transactions (timing differences).

(2) Delay in recording of bank transactions by customer (timing differences).

(3) Errors (by bank or customer).

Examples

➢ Unpresented cheques

➢ Outstanding lodgements   } Timing differences

➢ Bank interest/charges

➢ Standing orders ("SOs")

➢ Direct debits ("DDs")   Items on bank statement not in cash book

➢ Credit transfers

➢ Dishonoured cheques

➢ Bank errors

➢ Cash book (CB) errors

— cast errors

— transpositions

— omissions

— duplications

Reasons why a cheque may be dishonoured

✗ Payer does not have sufficient funds/overdraft facility.

✗ Post-dated or out of date (> 6 months).

✗ Discrepancy between amounts (narrative *vs* numerals).

✗ Account closed.

✗ Payer puts a "stop" on it.

1.4 Reconciliation procedure

Step 1   Correct/amend CB $\Rightarrow$ D/Es.
Step 2   Adjust bank statement balance for:
     —   timing differences
     —   bank errors.

1.5   Proforma XYZ Bank reconciliation as at ...

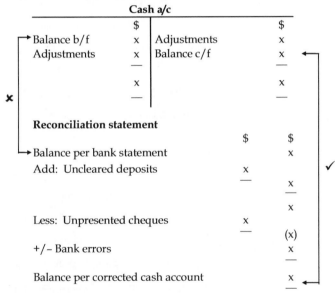

Cash a/c

	$		$
Balance b/f	x	Adjustments	x
Adjustments	x	Balance c/f	x
	x		x

Reconciliation statement

	$	$
Balance per bank statement		x
Add: Uncleared deposits	x	
		x
		x
Less: Unpresented cheques	x	
		(x)
+/– Bank errors		x
Balance per corrected cash account		x

SUMMARY

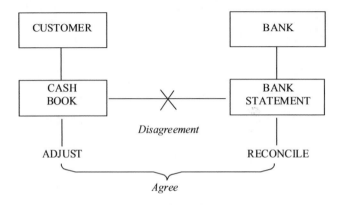

CUSTOMER   BANK

CASH BOOK   BANK STATEMENT

Disagreement

ADJUST   RECONCILE

Agree

1 ERRORS

1.1 ⇒ Difference = detected by TB

- ✓ Transposition (÷ 9).
- ✓ Other posting errors from books of prime entry.
- ✓ Single-sided entries.
- ✓ Two entries to same side.
- ✓ Addition (i.e. casting) errors in general ledger a/cs.
- ✓ Errors on b/f balances (e.g. omission, wrong amount/side).
- ✓ Errors of extraction (e.g. omission, wrong amount/side).

1.2 No difference = NOT detected by TB

- ✓ Errors of commission (to wrong account).
- ✓ Errors of (accounting) principle.
- ✓ Errors of omission (in book of prime entry).
- ✓ Compensating errors (rare).

1.3 Importance of ledger control a/cs

- ✓ If maintained in general ledger: error in individual account *cannot* affect balancing of TB.
- ✓ If *not* maintained: such errors may affect TB balance.

2 SUSPENSE ACCOUNTS

2.1 Why?

(1) To maintain D/E when destination of posting unknown.

(2) To record any difference on a TB. **Errors affecting the balance of the TB will be corrected against the suspense a/c** until it is cleared to zero

2.2 Correcting errors

- ✓ Suspense a/c entry is always *opposite* of correcting entry.

3 ADJUSTMENT TO PROFIT

3.1 Why?

- ✓ When further adjustments are required to a previously derived profit figure.

3.2 When?

- ✓ If, and only if, an adjustment affects the statement of financial position also.

3.3   How?

SUMMARY

**Statement of adjustments to profit
for the year ended . . . .**

	$	$	$
	−	+	
Profit per draft accounts			x
Accrued expenses	x		
Bad debt w/o	x		
Profit on sale of non-current asset		x	
	x	x	
		(x)	
			x/(x)
Adjusted profit			x

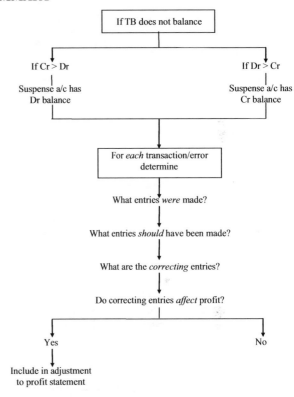

1 ACCOUNTING RECORDS

1.1 Include

✓ Books of prime entry.
✓ Ledgers.
✓ Inventory records and other asset registers.

Reason for keeping

✓ To comply with legislation/regulations.

✓ To produce financial statements.

✓ To control operations.

✓ To safeguard assets.

Reasons for not keeping

✓ No legal requirement.

✓ Cost of a bookkeeper is not justified.

✓ Information for preparing financial statements can be obtained from other sources.

1.2 Limited *v* incomplete accounting records

✓ Limited – transactions are recorded but further information is required to prepare financial statements.

✓ Incomplete – some transactions have not been recorded.

2 NET ASSETS APPROACH

2.1 Accounting equation

✓ Used when information is so scarce that a statement of profit or loss cannot be prepared:

> ➢ calculate opening net assets;
> ➢ prepare closing statement of financial position;
> ➢ use accounting equation.

Calculation of profit

	$	
Opening capital	x	
+ Capital introduced	x	
+/– Profit/Loss	x	(ßal)
– Drawings	(x)	
Closing capital	x	

✓ Also used to calculate drawings.

3 CASH BOOK APPROACH

3.1 Cash and bank

✓ Cash a/c used to record movements in/out of cash register.

✓ Bankings will be known (recorded on bank statement):

✓ Dr   Bank
   Cr   Cash

✓ Possible reasons for balancing figure on cash a/c:

   ➢ drawings by proprietor;
   ➢ cash receipts stolen (after being recorded);
   ➢ unrecorded cash receipts (which have been banked).

3.2 Control accounts

✓ Use to find balancing figure, e.g.:

   ➢ lost/unrecorded sales/purchase invoices;
   ➢ cash stolen from receipts from customers;
   ➢ total sales/purchases.

3.3 Cost structures

*Gross profit percentage (% **on** sales revenue)*

$$\frac{\text{Gross profit}}{\text{Revenue}} \times 100$$

*"Mark-up" (% **on** cost)*

$$\frac{\text{Gross profit}}{\text{Cost of sales}} \times 100$$

3.4 Combining techniques

✓ Trade payables ledger control a/c $\Rightarrow$ Purchases.

✓ Purchases + inventory movement $\Rightarrow$ Cost of sales.

✓ Cost of sales + cost structure $\Rightarrow$ Sales revenue.

✓ Sales revenue into trade receivables ledger control a/c $\Rightarrow$ Cash receipts.

✓ Cash receipts into cash book $\Rightarrow$ Drawings!

1 IFRC FOUNDATION

1.1 About the Foundation

✓ Independent body oversees IASB.

✓ Committed to developing (in public interest):
a *single set* of high quality, understandable and enforceable
global accounting standards requiring
transparent and *comparable* information in
general purpose financial statements*.

* i.e. to meet needs of users not in a position to demand reports for specific information needs

✓ IASB co-operates with accounting standard-setters to achieve convergence world-wide.

1.2 IASB objectives

✓ To develop … (see "Committed to …" at §1.1 above).

✓ To promote use and rigorous application.

✓ To take account of needs of SMEs/emerging economies.

✓ To promote and facilitate adoption, through convergence.

1.3 Constitution

Structure

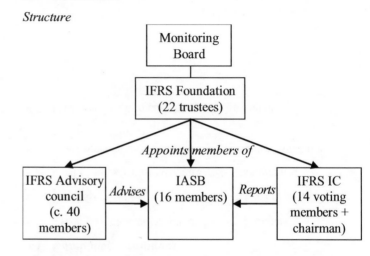

IFRS Foundation trustees

✓ Appointed by independent "nominating committee".
✓ Individuals from professional backgrounds.

1.4 IASB

✓ An independent private sector body.
✓ Sole body with responsibility and authority to issue pronouncements (IFRSs).

Agenda

- ✓ Full discretion in developing technical agenda for standard setting.

- ✓ Publications require approval of 10 of 16 members.

1.5 IFRS Advisory Council

- ✓ A forum for participation by interested parties (e.g. OECD, FASB, EC).

- ✓ Advises IASB on:
  - ➤ agenda issues
  - ➤ work priorities
  - ➤ views on major standard-setting projects.

1.6 IFRS Interpretations Committee

Responsibilities

- ✓ Interpreting application of IFRSs.

- ✓ Providing timely guidance on financial reporting issues not specifically addressed in IFRSs.

- ✓ Publish Draft Interpretations for public comment (after clearance by IASB).

- ✓ Obtain board approval for final interpretations.

2 IFRSs

2.1 Development of IFRSs

IASB

- ✓ Consults with Advisory Council (in public meetings) on:
  - ➤ major projects;
  - ➤ agenda decisions;
  - ➤ work priorities.

- ✓ Discusses technical matters in public meetings.

"Due process"

- ✓ Identify/review issues and consider "Framework".

- ✓ Exchange views with national standard setters.

- ✓ Consult with IFRS Advisory Council to include topic in IASB's agenda.

- ✓ Form advisory ("working") group.

- ✓ Publish Discussion Paper (DP) for public comment.

- ✓ Publish Exposure Draft (ED) for public comment.

- ✓ Consider comments received/revise documents if necessary.

- ✓ Consider holding public hearing/field tests.

- ✓ Deliberate costs and benefits.

- ✓ Approve and publish.

Overview

STEERING COMMITEE	BOARD	STANDARDS ADVISORY COMMITEE

←advise

Develop and publish DP

Develop and publish ED ← Public comment

Issue final standard

Feedback Statement

2.2 Steps to achieve consistent interpretation

✓ "Annual improvements project".
✓ Publication of a "statement of principles".
✓ "Updates" – staff summaries of developments.
✓ Issue of Interpretations by IFRS IC.

2.3 Scope and application

✓ All published financial statements of entities with profit motive.

✓ Separate and consolidated financial statements.

✗ Do **not** apply to immaterial items.

✗ **Not** retroactive from date specified (unless stated otherwise).

Exclusions

✗ Non-business entities.
✗ Private sector NFP entities.

2.4 Harmonisation

Is achieved where:

✓ Adopted as national requirements.
✓ Used as basis for national requirements.
✓ Used as international benchmark.
✓ Incorporated in legislation.

3 CORPORATE GOVERNANCE

3.1 Meaning

The system by which entities are directed and controlled ... specifies the distribution of rights and responsibilities ... how objectives are set and attained, risks monitored and performance optimised.

✓ Encourages value creation, accountability and control.

3.2 In the context of preparing financial statements

UK Corporate Governance Code

✓ **Board** must present a balanced and understandable set of financial statements and maintain a sound system of internal control (including risk management).

✓ An **audit committee** must:

➢ monitor the integrity of the financial statements;
➢ review internal controls/risk management systems;
➢ monitor the internal and external auditors.

3.3 Directors' collective duties and responsibilities

✓ For "a true and fair view". Includes:

➢ compliance with law and GAAP;
➢ adequate account records.

✓ Presentation to, and approval by, shareholders.

Accounting records

Must be adequate:

✓ To show and explain transactions.

✓ To disclose financial position (with reasonable accuracy, at any time).

✓ To prepare accounts to comply with legal requirements.

✓ To show, daily, all receipts and payments.

✓ To record assets and liabilities.

3.4 Audit committee responsibilities

✓ To ensure shareholders' interests are properly protected.

✓ To monitor integrity of financial statements, etc.

✓ To review internal controls and risk management.

✓ To review and monitor effectiveness of auditors (internal and external).

✓ To review and monitor independence and objectivity of external auditor.

1 DEFINITION, PURPOSE AND STATUS

A statement of generally accepted **assumptions and principles ...** provides a frame of **reference** for developing new practices and evaluating existing ones.

1.1 Purpose

✓ Principally, to assist the Board of IASB in:

  ➢ developing IFRSs;
  ➢ promoting harmonisation.

✓ To assist:

  ➢ national standard setting bodies;
  ➢ preparers of financial statements;
  ➢ auditors in forming an opinion;
  ➢ users in interpreting financial information.

1.2 Status

The Framework is **not** an IFRS and does **not** define standards for specific measurement or disclosure.

✓ Nothing in it can override a specific IAS.

✓ In case of conflict a standard prevails.

1.3 Financial statements

✓ Statement of financial position ("balance sheet").
✓ Statement of comprehensive income.
✓ Statement of cash flows.
✓ Statement of changes in equity (SoCIE);
✓ Integral notes, other statements, explanatory material.

These are described in IAS 1 (see next section).

1.4 Application

✓ Financial statements of all commercial/industrial/ business entities, (public or private).

2 GENERAL PURPOSE FINANCIAL STATEMENTS

2.1 Objective

✓ To provide information ... useful to a wide range of users in making economic decisions.

✓ Also, to show management's stewardship.

2.2 Limitations

✘ Cannot meet all information needs.
✘ Aimed at primary users (i.e. shareholders).
✘ Do not show entity's "worth".
✘ Based extensively on estimates, judgements, models.

2.3 Information

✓ Helps users to evaluate:

> ➢ ability to generate cash and cash equivalents;
> ➢ timing and certainty of their generation.

Financial position

✓ "Economic resources" (assets) controlled.
✓ "Claims" (liabilities).
✓ Financial structure.
✓ Liquidity and solvency.
✓ Capacity to adapt to changes.

Financial performance

✓ Profitability.
✓ Capacity to generate cash from existing resources.
✓ Effectiveness with which additional resources might be employed.

Changes in financial position

✓ Investing, financing and operating activities.
✓ Ability to generate cash and use of cash.

Accrual accounting

… provides a better basis for assessing performance than cash receipts and payments.

✓ Effects of transactions and other events:

> ➢ recognised when they occur (**not** when cash received/paid);
> ➢ recorded in accounting records and reported in financial statements in period to which they relate.

2.4 Underlying assumption – Going concern

… entity will continue in operation for *foreseeable future*.

✓ Assumption about *continuity* is reflected in monetary values.
✓ No intention/necessity to liquidate/significantly curtail scale of operations.
✓ Use of different basis (e.g. "break-up") is **rare**.

3   QUALITATIVE CHARACTERISTICS

Attributes that make information useful to users.

3.1 Economic phenomena

✓ **Transactions**, **conditions** and other **events** that affect economic resources and claims against the entity.

3.2 Fundamental qualitative characteristics

✓ **Relevance** and **faithful representation**.

Enhancing characteristics

✓ Comparability
✓ Verifiability
✓ Timeliness
✓ Understandability.

3.3 Relevance

✓ Helps users:

> ➤ evaluate past, present or future events; and
> ➤ confirm or correct past evaluations.

✓ Relevance of information is affected by:

> ➤ nature (alone may be insufficient to be relevant);
> ➤ materiality.

Materiality

"Information is material if its omission or misstatement could influence the economic decisions of users taken on the basis of the financial statements."

✓ Depends on size ... omission or misstatement.

✓ A "threshold" or "cut-off point" (not a primary qualitative characteristic).

3.4 Faithful representation

✓ For example, assets meet recognition criteria.

Qualities

✓ Neutrality (free from *material* bias).
✓ Completeness (within bounds of materiality and cost).
✓ Accuracy (free from *material* error).

3.5 Cost constraint

✓ Cost of information should not exceed benefit.

4 ELEMENTS OF FINANCIAL STATEMENTS

Broad classes of financial effects grouped according to economic characteristics.

4.1 Definitions

✓ Asset:

> ➤ resource *controlled*;
> ➤ result of *past* events;
> ➤ *future economic benefits* expected to flow.

✓ Liability:

> ➤ *present obligation*;
> ➤ results of *past* events;
> ➤ expected to result in an *outflow of resources*.

- ✓ Equity:
  - ➢ residual interest in assets;
  - ➢ after deducting all liabilities.

- ✓ Income:
  - ➢ increases in economic benefits;
  - ➢ inflows of assets or decreases of liabilities;
  - ➢ result in increase in equity;
  - ➢ excluding contributions from equity participants.

- ✓ Expenses:
  - ➢ decreases in economic benefits;
  - ➢ outflows of assets or incurrences of liabilities;
  - ➢ result in decreases in equity;
  - ➢ excluding distributions to equity participants.

4.2 "Substance over form"

- ✓ Looks at economic reality not merely legal form (e.g. to assess whether definitions of elements are met).

- ✓ Differences between substance and form may compromise faithful representation.

4.3 Recognition

Meaning

- ✓ To incorporate an item that:
  - ➢ meets **definition** of an element; and
  - ➢ satisfies recognition **criteria**.

- ✓ Depiction in words and monetary amount (and inclusion in totals).

- ✘ Failure to recognise items is **not** rectified by disclosure of accounting policies, notes or explanatory material.

Criteria

- ✓ **Probable** future economic benefit (to or from entity); and

- ✓ **Reliable measurement** of cost/value.

1 SCOPE

1.1 General purpose financial statements

Meaning

✓ Intended to meet needs of users not in a position to demand tailored reports.

✓ Usually presented in an annual report.

1.2 Application of IAS 1

✓ To separate and consolidated financial statements.
✓ All commercial entities (including banks, etc).
✓ Entities with profit objective (including public sector).

2 FINANCIAL STATEMENTS

A *structured* representation of financial position and financial performance.

2.1 Objective

See "Framework".

Responsibility for preparation and presentation

Board of directors and/or governing body (i.e. management).

2.2 Components

✓ See "Framework".

Significant accounting policies and other explanatory notes are integral.

✘ Non-financial statements (see *section 1*).

2.3 Supplementary statements

✓ Additional voluntary information (e.g. management review, environmental reports).

Are outside scope of IFRSs.

3 GENERAL FEATURES

3.1 Fair presentation and compliance with IFRS

✓ Achieved by appropriate application of IFRS (additional disclosure if needed).

✓ Compliance with IFRS **must** be disclosed.

✘ Inappropriate accounting treatment is **not** rectified by:

➤ disclosure of accounting policies;
➤ notes or explanatory material.

If compliance would be misleading (*extremely* rare) departure must be disclosed (nature and financial impact).

3.2 Going concern

✓ Management's responsibility to:

➢ assess ability to continue as a going concern;

➢ prepare financial statements on going concern basis (unless inappropriate);

➢ disclose material uncertainties that may affect assumption.

✓ Disclose, with reasons, if financial statements prepared on a different basis.

"Foreseeable future"

✓ Normally at least, but not limited to, 12 months after reporting period.

3.3 Accrual basis of accounting

Financial statements (except statement of cash flows) should be prepared under accruals basis.

Concept

✓ See "Framework".

"Matching" concept

✓ Expenses are recognised on basis of a *direct association* between:

➢ costs incurred; and
➢ specific earning.

3.4 Materiality and aggregation

✓ See also *Framework*.
✓ If material – present separately.
✓ If immaterial – aggregate.

3.5 Offsetting

✗ NO offsetting unless required or permitted by IFRS.

Permitted

✓ Netting off gains/losses on non-current asset disposals.

✓ Reporting assets net of valuation allowances is **not** offsetting.

3.6 Frequency of reporting

✓ At least annually.

✓ If end of the reporting period is changed disclose:

➢ reason for period being other than one year;
➢ fact that corresponding amounts are not entirely comparable.

3.7 Comparative information

✓ Numerical information – disclose unless IFRS permits/requires otherwise.

✓ Narrative information – include only if relevant to understanding *current* period.

3.8 Consistency of presentation

Presentation and classification of items should be retained from one period to the next.

Exceptions

✓ Change (voluntary) ⇒ more appropriate presentation.
✓ Change (mandatory) is required by IFRS.

4 STRUCTURE AND CONTENT

4.1 "Disclosure"

✓ Encompassing items presented in each financial statement as well as notes.

4.2 Identification of financial statements

Must be clearly identified and distinguished from other information (e.g. in annual report)

Information to be prominently displayed

✓ Component presented.
✓ Name of reporting entity.
✓ Whether individual entity or group.
✓ End of the reporting period ("reporting date") or period covered.
✓ Presentation currency.
✓ Level of precision (e.g. 000).

5 STATEMENT OF FINANCIAL POSITION

5.1 Current/non-current distinction

✓ "Non-current" – tangible, intangible, operating and financial assets of long-term nature.

Current assets

✓ Expected to be realised/intended for sale or consumption in normal course of operating cycle.

✓ Held primarily for trading purposes.

✓ Expected to be realised <12 months after reporting period.

✓ Cash or a cash equivalent.

Classify all other assets as "non-current".

5.2 Current liabilities

✓ Expected to be settled in normal course of the operating cycle.

✓ Held primarily for trading purposes.

✓ Due to be settled < 12 months after reporting period.

✓ A liability payable on demand is current.

Classify all other liabilities as "non-current".

5.3 Line items

Minimum requirements

✓ Property, plant and equipment
✓ Intangible assets
✓ Investments
✓ Inventories
✓ Trade and other receivables
✓ Cash and cash equivalents
✓ Trade and other payables
✓ Current tax liabilities
✓ Provisions
✓ Issued equity capital and reserves
✓ Non-controlling interest.

5.4 Proforma

✓ Essentially the minimum line items per IAS 1.

5.5 Other information

✓ Intangibles (per IAS 38).
✓ Tangible assets by class (per IAS 16)
✓ Receivables – trade customers and prepayments.
✓ Inventories (per IAS 2).

Shareholders' interests

✓ Equity capital and reserves:

➢ classes of paid in capital;
➢ share premium;
➢ reserves.

✓ For each class of share capital:

➢ number of shares authorised;
➢ number of shares issued;
➢ par ("nominal") value per share (or no par value);
➢ rights, preferences and restrictions on dividends;
➢ a reconciliation of number (start and end of year).

✓ Nature and purpose of each reserve (e.g. revaluation surplus, share premium).

6 STATEMENT OF COMPREHENSIVE INCOME

6.1 Format

✓ In a *single* statement of comprehensive income; or

✓ In *two* statements:

   ➤ profit or loss; and
   ➤ components of other comprehensive income.

6.2 Minimum line items

✓ Revenue
✓ Finance costs
✓ Tax expense
✓ Profit or loss (excluding other comprehensive income)
✓ Each component of other comprehensive income
✓ Total comprehensive income.

Dividends

✘ Appropriations are **not** shown in statements of comprehensive income.

Material items

✓ Disclose separately (additional line items) – nature and amount (e.g. write-downs).

✘ **NO** "extraordinary" items.

6.3 Analysis of expenses

Nature (not allocated to functions)

✓ Depreciation
✓ Purchases of materials
✓ Transport costs
✓ Wages and salaries
✓ Advertising costs.

Advantages

✓ Easier to prepare (smaller entities).
✓ No arbitrary allocations between functions.
✓ More objective (little judgement).
✓ Facilitates more meaningful comparison.

Cost of sales method

✓ Cost of sales
✓ Distribution
✓ Administrative activities.

Advantage

✓ Provides more relevant information.

Disadvantage

✘ Arbitrary cost allocation
✘ Involves considerable judgement.

6.4 Proformas

By function	By nature
✓ **Revenue**	✓ **Revenue**
✓ Cost of sales	✓ Other operating income
✓ Gross profit/(loss)	✓ Changes in inventories
✓ Other income	✓ Work capitalised
✓ Distribution costs	✓ Raw materials/ consumables used
✓ Administrative expenses	✓ Staff costs
	✓ Depreciation/amortisation

Otherwise the same:

- ✓ Finance costs
- ✓ Share of profit or associates
- ✓ Income tax expense
- ✓ Other comprehensive income (itemised).

6.5 Income tax

- ✓ Liability estimated at end of financial year.
- ✓ Actual amount usually different.
- ✓ Under/over provision is a change in estimate in year of payment.

7 STATEMENT OF CHANGES IN EQUITY ("SoCIE")

7.1 Separate statement shows

✓ Total comprehensive income for period.

✓ Transactions with owners (contributions and distributions).

✓ A reconciliation of carrying amounts (beginning and end) for each component.

7.2 Proforma

✓ Column for each component – totalled.

✓ Full comparative information.

8 NOTES TO THE FINANCIAL STATEMENTS

8.1 Information

✓ About items that do not qualify for recognition.

✓ Narrative descriptions and disaggregations.

✓ Basis of preparation.

✓ Specific accounting policies.

✓ Information required by IFRSs not presented elsewhere.

✓ Additional information necessary for "fair presentation".

Presentation

✓ Systematic manner.

✓ Cross-referenced to notes.

Normal order

Assists users (e.g. to make comparisons with other entities):

✓ Compliance with IFRS;

✓ Measurement basis and accounting policies;

✓ Supporting information;

✓ Other disclosures:

➤ contingencies, capital commitments, etc;
➤ non-financial.

8.2 Disclosure of accounting policies

Matters described

✓ Measurement basis (or bases) used (e.g. historical cost, fair value).

✓ Each specific accounting policy.

✓ Significant judgements made by management in applying accounting policies.

Accounting policies considered

✓ Revenue recognition (IAS 18)

✓ Recognition and depreciation/amortisation of tangible (IAS 16) and intangible assets (IAS 38)

✓ Research and development costs (IAS 38).

✓ Inventories (IAS 2).

✓ Provisions (IAS 37).

8.3 Other disclosures in notes

Dividends

✓ Amounts proposed or declared but **not** recognised as a distribution during the period.

✓ Amounts for cumulative preference shares not recognised.

Entity

✓ Domicile and legal form.

✓ Country of incorporation

✓ Description of nature of operations/principal activities.

✓ Name of parent/ultimate parent.

1 LIMITED LIABILITY COMPANY

1.1 Key features

Business entity concept

- ✓ Incorporated enterprise = an artificial legal person (i.e. "separate legal entity").

- ✓ Can sue and be sued.

- ✓ Can contract in own name.

- ✓ Is not affected by change in ownership.

Shareholders

- ✓ Owners of shares.

Limited liability

- ✓ Entity is liable to pay up to total net assets of owners.

- ✓ **Shareholders** liability is limited to amounts paid in/to be paid in.

Management (e.g. directors)

- ✓ Appointed by shareholders to manage entity on their behalf.

1.2 Advantages

- ✓ Limited liability.

- ✓ Business entity concept $\Rightarrow$ less risk to owners.

- ✓ Shareholding less cumbersome than partnership.

- ✓ Shares more easily transferred.

- ✓ May be tax advantages.

- ✓ Commercial credibility of company status.

- ✓ Increased access to sources of finance.

1.3 Disadvantages

- ✗ Formation costs (though not prohibitive).

- ✗ Compliance costs (e.g. annual audit, accounting returns, etc).

- ✗ Responsibility and control delegated to management.

- ✗ Difficult to return capital to shareholders (on winding up).

- ✗ May be tax disadvantages.

- ✗ Loss of privacy of information due to disclosure requirements.

2 CAPITAL STRUCTURE

The particular combination of equity (shares) and loans (debt) and other sources of long-term finance.

2.1 Major sources

Share capital	*Other*
✓ Ordinary shares ("equity").	✓ Loan notes/bonds.
✓ Preferred shares (treated as "debt" under IFRS).	✓ Bank loans and overdrafts.
✓ Return dividends (but under IFRS preference dividends are treated as interest).	✓ Also trade payables.
	✓ Interest is an *expense* to profit or loss.
✓ Dividends on ordinary shares are an *appropriation of profit.*	

Debt security

✓ Fixed charges on pledged assets (e.g. by mortgage).
✓ Floating charges over changing assets (e.g. inventory).
✓ Unsecured.

2.2 Types of shares

Ordinary shares	*Preference shares*
✓ Higher return (uncertain) for higher risk.	✓ Lower return (certain) for lower risk.
✓ Carry voting rights.	✓ Mostly non-voting.
✓ Varying dividends (non-cumulative).	✓ Fixed dividends (% of par value) accumulate (if unpaid).
✓ Participation in surplus on liquidation.	✓ Usually no participation in surplus.
	✓ May be redeemable.
	✓ May be convertible to equity.

3 SHARE CAPITAL

3.1 Meaning

✓ Ownership of *ordinary* shares gives rights to share of:
  ➢ profits;
  ➢ assets (in event of winding up).
✓ *Preference* share capital is debt (under IFRS) if redeemable.

Preference shares	*v*	*Ordinary shares*

✓ Fixed rate dividends have prior claim on distributable profits.

✓ Entitled to remaining profits (when declared).

Bonus ("scrip") issue	*v*	*Rights issue*

✓ NO CASH;

✓ Capitalisation of reserves;

✓ To existing share-holders "pro-rata".

✓ First offered to existing share-holders pro-rata;

✓ Often at price < MV;

✓ Shareholders can sell rights to others;

✓ All pay CASH.

Market value (MV):	*v*	*Nominal ("par") value*

✓ Reflects perceived MV of business;

✓ Price quoted on Stock Exchange.

✓ Stated (i.e. "book") value;

✓ Used to calculate dividends.

3.2 Issue

✓ At NV: Dr Cash
　　　　　　Cr Share capital

✓ At > MV: Dr Cash
　　　　　　Cr Share capital
　　　　　　Cr Share premium

✗ At < MV: prohibited.

✓ Bonus issue:

　　　Dr Retained earnings/Share premium
　　　　Cr Share capital (NV)

3.3 Relative advantages

Bonus issue	*Rights issue*
✓ Can change structure of share capital (e.g. distributable profits $\Rightarrow$ equity shares).	✓ Raises capital and cash.
✓ MV per share falls (not necessarily pro rata).	✓ Cheapest way of raising equity finance.
✓ Signals strength to stock market.	✓ More likely to be successful than new issue to public.

4 RESERVES

4.1 Capital reserves

✓ Non-distributable.

✓ Examples:

> ➤ Share premium;
> ➤ Revaluation.

Share premium

✗ **Not** distributable (it is capital not profit).

✓ Limited uses:

> ➤ issue of fully-paid bonus shares;
> ➤ paying preliminary expenses on company formation;
> ➤ paying premium to redeem shares or bonds.

Revaluation surplus

✓ An *unrealised* gain on revalued non-current assets.

✗ **Cannot** be used for dividend payment until realised.

✓ Can be used to finance bonus shares (deemed to be paid in full).

4.2 Revenue reserves

✓ Are distributable.

✓ Principally retained earnings.

✓ Other:

> ➤ Asset replacement;
> ➤ General.

Retained earnings

✓ Accumulated unappropriated profits retained for reinvestment in operations.

✓ Later dividends may be paid out of retained profits.

✓ Amounts may be transferred to other named reserves (e.g. for asset replacement).

✓ When a revalued asset is sold the revaluation surplus is "realised" and transferred to retained earnings (in SoCIE).

5 COST OF CAPITAL

5.1 Dividends

✓ Appropriations of distributable profits in proportion to shareholdings.

✓ Are *proposed* by the management and *approved* ("declared") by company in general meeting.

✓ Expressed as:

➢ a % (e.g. preference shares);
➢ an amount per share (e.g. ordinary shares).

Accounting entries

✓ When a dividend on equity shares is declared (i.e. becomes a legal liability):

    Dr   Retained earnings
       Cr   Dividends payable (current liability)

✓ When paid:

    Dr   Dividends payable
       Cr   Cash

✓ Under IFRS preference dividends are an interest **expense** in profit or loss.

Disclosure (IAS 1)

✓ Amount of dividends in *total* and *per share* in SoCIE (or notes).

5.2 Finance costs

✓ Includes all costs arising from financing transactions.

Examples

✓ Costs relating loans/borrowings (e.g. interest, late payment penalties).

✓ Preference dividends.

✓ Finance costs implicit in lease payments (not examinable).

✓ Costs of "factoring" debts (not examinable).

Accounting entries

✓ When incurred (i.e. becomes a legal liability):

    Dr   Finance cost (e.g. interest)
       Cr   Interest payable (current liability)

✓ When paid:

    Dr   Interest payable
       Cr   Cash

1   IAS 2

1.1   Definitions

Inventories are assets:

- ✓ held for resale in ordinary course of business;
- ✓ in the process of production for resale;
- ✓ consumables supplies.

Net realisable value (NRV)

- ✓ Estimated selling price in ordinary course of business *less* estimated cost of completion/ sale.

2   MEASUREMENT

- ✓ At the **lower** of *cost* and *net realisable value*.

2.1   Cost

All *costs of purchase* (net of trade discounts) and *conversion* (including overheads) and other costs involved in bringing inventories to present location and condition.

Expenditures **excluded**:

- ✗ abnormal waste/losses, etc;
- ✗ storage (unless part of production process);
- ✗ administrative overheads; and
- ✗ selling costs.

2.2   Measurement techniques

- ✓ For approximation of *actual* cost:

Standard cost	Retail method
✓ At normal levels of materials, labour, efficiency and capacity.	✓ For numerous product lines with similar margins.
✓ Must be kept up-to-date.	✓ Sales value less % gross margin.
✓ May need to be adapted to conform to IAS 2.	✓ Practical in retail industry.

2.3   Cost formulas

Specific identification of individual costs

- ✓ Items **not** ordinarily interchangeable.
- ✓ Goods/services produced and segregated for specific projects.

Formulae

- ✓ Permitted where specific identification of individual costs is not practicable.

- ✓ Inventories **must** be "ordinarily interchangeable".

First-in, first-out (FIFO)	*Weighted average (WAC)*
✓ Items purchased/ manufactured first are sold first. ✓ Inventory at period end is most recently purchased/ produced. ✓ Examples: ➢ cars on a production line; ➢ retail produce with "sell by"/ "best before" date.	✓ WAC (AVCO) of: ➢ opening inventory; and ➢ similar items purchased/ produced in period. ✓ Calculated periodically or on each purchase/ production. ✓ Used when like items are produced/sold disregarding date of purchase/ manufacture.

Accounting policies

✓ **Consistency:** The same accounting policy should be applied to similar items (by category).

3 NET REALISABLE VALUE

3.1 Need for

Reasons why costs may not be recoverable

✗ Damage.

✗ Obsolescence.

✗ Falling selling price.

✗ Increasing estimated costs to completion.

3.2 Core principle

✓ Inventories cannot be carried in excess of amounts expected to be realised from their sale or use ("prudence" concept).

Application

✓ Write down is usually on an item-by-item basis ("offset" concept).

3.3 Estimating NRV

Considerations

✓ Fluctuations of price/cost relating to events after the period end.

✓ Purpose for which inventory is held.

Raw materials

✓ Only (rarely) written down to below cost when cost of finished products would exceed NRV.

Timing

✓ At end of each reporting period.

✓ On subsequent review must *reverse* write-down (if circumstances causing write-down no longer exist).

4 RECOGNITION AND DISCLOSURE

4.1 Recognition as an expense

✓ Usually called "cost of sales".

✓ Carrying amount of inventories sold is expensed in the period in which related revenue is recognised ("accruals" concept).

✓ Write-downs are expensed in period when recognised.

✓ Reversals are recognised as a *reduction* in expense in the period the reversal occurs. (A change in accounting estimate.)

✓ Inventories capitalised (e.g. in self-constructed assets) are expensed over the useful life of the asset (within depreciation).

4.2 Disclosure

✓ Accounting policies – including cost formula(s) used.

Carrying amounts

✓ Total – with appropriate sub-classifications (e.g. raw materials, goods for resale).

✓ Carrying amount at fair value less costs to sell.

✓ Carrying amount of inventories pledged as security for liabilities.

Separate disclosure

✓ Any write-down "of such size, incidence or nature" requires separate disclosure.

1 PRINCIPLES OF REVENUE RECOGNITION

1.1 IFRS 15

1. Identify the contract(s) with the customer.

2. Identify separate performance obligations.

3. Determine transaction price.

4. Allocate transaction price to performance obligations.

5. Recognise revenue when (or as) performance obligation is satisfied.

! At the amount of consideration **expected** to be received.

1.2 Criteria

✓ Contract is **approved**.

✓ **Rights** (to goods or services) are identified.

✓ **Payment** terms are stated.

✓ Contract has **commercial substance**

✓ **Consideration** due is expected to be collected.

! **All** criteria must be met.

1.3 Performance obligations

✓ A promise to transfer:

➤ a good or service that is **distinct**; or

➤ a series of goods or services that are substantially the same and transferred in the same way.

✓ A good or service is distinct if:

➤ the customer can benefit from it on its own or when combined with available resources; **and**

➤ the promise to transfer it is separately identifiable in the contract.

1.4 Transaction price

✓ The amount of consideration in exchange for the transfer.

✓ Is allocated to separate obligations in proportion to stand-alone selling prices.

1.5 Recognise revenue

✓ When performance obligation is satisfied:

➤ Over time (e.g. a service);

➤ At a point in time (e.g. when customer obtains control of the asset).

---

1   IAS 16

1.1   Terminology

✓   See page 0901, also …

✓   *Impairment loss* – excess of carrying amount over recoverable amount.

✓   *Recoverable amount* – **higher** of "fair value less costs to sell" and "value in use".

1.2   Recognition criteria

✓   As per "Framework":

➢   *probable* future economic benefits; and
➢   cost can be measured reliably.

2   MEASUREMENT

2.1   Initially at cost

Components

✓   Purchase price (net of trade discount).
✓   Directly attributable costs (delivery, installation, etc).
✓   An *initial* estimate of decommissioning cost (a liability).

Exchange of assets

✓   Fair value of asset received = Fair value of the asset given up ± cash element.

2.2   Subsequent costs

✓   Servicing/repairs and maintenance – expensed to profit or loss as incurred.

3   SUBSEQUENT MEASUREMENT

3.1   Accounting policies

✓   *Cost* model or *revaluation* model.
✓   Applied to each item in a *class* of assets.

3.2   Carrying amount

✓   **Cost model:** cost – accumulated depreciation – accumulated impairment losses.

✓   **Revaluation model:** revalued amount – accumulated depreciation – accumulated impairment losses.

4   REVALUATIONS

4.1   Fair values

✓   Reliable measurement is **essential**.

✓   Land and buildings – market value.

✓   Plant and equipment – usually:

➢   market value (appraised); or
➢   depreciated replacement cost.

4.2 Frequency

✓ Sufficiently regularly (so no material difference between carrying amount and fair value).

✓ May be on "rolling" basis (entire class).

4.3 Accumulated depreciation

✓ Two methods:

➢ restate proportionately;
➢ "eliminate" against gross carrying amount (and restate net).

4.4 Movement

✓ Increase ⇒ other comprehensive income (accumulated in equity as "revaluation surplus").

✓ Decrease:

⇒ expense in profit or loss; or
⇒ other comprehensive income (if reversing previous gain).

4.5 Subsequent accounting

Transfer to retained earnings

✓ Is allowed but not required:

➢ Annually (depreciation difference);
➢ On disposal.

✘ Must **not** be "recycled" through profit or loss.

5 DEPRECIATION

5.1 Accounting standards

✓ Systematic basis over *useful life*.

✓ Method to reflect consumption of economic benefits.

✓ Depreciation charge to be expenses (unless a cost of another asset).

5.2 Useful life – factors

✓ Land – unlimited (is not depreciable).

✓ All other assets:

➢ expected usage;
➢ expected physical wear and tear;
➢ technical obsolescence;
➢ legal or similar limits on use;
➢ asset management policy;
➢ repair and maintenance policy.

5.3 Residual value

- ✓ Often immaterial.
- ✓ If > carrying amount depreciation charge is zero.

5.4 Depreciation period

- ✓ Commences when asset is available for use.
- ✓ Ceases when an asset is derecognised.

5.5 Methods

- ✓ Straight-line ⇒ constant charge.

- ✓ Reducing (diminishing) balance ⇒ a decreasing charge.

- ✓ Units of production ⇒ charge based on expected use/production output.

- ✓ Review periodically: Any change in method is a change in **accounting estimate**.

6 DERECOGNITION

6.1 Accounting treatment

- ✓ Statement of financial position: eliminate on disposal or abandonment.

- ✓ Profit or loss: gain or loss = difference between net disposal proceeds and carrying amount.

- ✓ Gains are not revenue.

7 DISCLOSURES

7.1 Each class

- ✓ Measurement bases.

- ✓ Depreciation methods.

- ✓ Useful lives or depreciation rates.

- ✓ Gross carrying amount and accumulated depreciation at beginning and end of period.

- ✓ Reconciliation of carrying amount at beginning and end of period showing movements.

7.2 Other

- ✓ Restrictions on title/assets pledged as security.
- ✓ Accounting policy for estimating restoration costs.
- ✓ Expenditure on assets in the course of construction.
- ✓ Contractual commitments.

7.3 Revalued items

- ✓ Effective date of revaluation.

- ✓ Whether independent valuer involved.

- ✓ Methods and significant assumptions applied to estimate fair values.

- ✓ Surplus – movements and restrictions on distribution.

1   INTANGIBLE ASSETS

Identifiable, non-monetary asset without physical substance.

1.1   Examples

✓ Computer software
✓ Patents and copyrights
✓ Licences and franchises
✓ Intellectual property
✓ Brand names.

2   GOODWILL

2.1   Definition

Future economic benefits deriving from assets that are not capable of individual identification and separate recognition.

✓ The difference between cost of acquiring a business and fair value of identifiable assets and liabilities acquired.

✓ Must be written down for subsequent impairment.

✗ Can **never** be revalued (upwards).

2.2   Two types

✓ Acquired/purchased – as results of purchase transaction.
✗ Internally-generated ("inherent") – cannot be recognised (no reliable measurement).

2.3   Purchased

✓ Recognised as an asset ("capitalised").

✓ Carried at cost but subject to annual impairment review.

Impairment of goodwill is **not** examinable.

3   RESEARCH AND DEVELOPMENT

3.1   Classification

✓ "Research phase" or "development phase".

✓ If indistinguishable treat as research phase.

3.2   Definitions

Research – original and planned investigation ... to gain *new* scientific or technical knowledge ...

Development – *application* of research findings to a plan to produce new or substantially improved materials, products, etc before commencing commercial production or use.

3.3   Initial measurement

✓ At cost = total expenditure incurred *after* recognition criteria met.

✗ Expenditure previously recognised is **not** reinstated.

4 RESEARCH EXPENDITURES

4.1 Accounting standard

✓ *Not* an intangible asset.

✓ Expenditure is recognised when incurred. Specifically including:

- ➤ start-up costs;
- ➤ training;
- ➤ advertising/promotion;
- ➤ relocation.

5 DEVELOPMENT EXPENDITURES

5.1 Accounting standard

✓ Intangible asset must be recognised if **all** asset recognition criteria **demonstrated.**

5.2 Criteria

✓ Technical feasibility of completing.
✓ Intention to complete and use/sell.
✓ Ability to use or sell.
✓ Existence of market for output/internal use.
✓ Adequate resources to complete and use/sell.
✓ Reliable measurement of attributable expenses.

5.3 Amortisation

✓ As for depreciation (IAS 16).

Method

✓ Should reflect pattern of consumption.
✓ Otherwise use straight-line.

5.4 Residual value

✓ Assumed to be *zero* unless there is:

- ➤ a third party commitment to purchase it; or
- ➤ an active market for it (unlikely).

6 DISCLOSURES

6.1 By class

✓ Similar to IAS 16.

6.2 Other

✓ *Aggregate* research and expenditure expense recognised in period.

6.3 Descriptions encouraged

✓ Fully amortised asset still in use.

✓ *Significant* intangible assets not recognised (i.e. not meeting recognition criteria).

1 IAS 37

1.1 Definitions

Provision

✓ Liabilities of uncertain timing or amount.

Liability

✓ A present obligation arising from past events (settlement of which is expected to result in an outflow of resources embodying economic benefits).

Contingent liability

✓ A possible obligation arising from past events ... **existence** will be confirmed by occurrence/non-occurrence of uncertain future event(s) not wholly within the entity's control; or

✓ A *present obligation* arising from *past* events (an "obligating event") that is *not recognised* because:

   ➤ an outflow of resources is *not probable*; or
   ➤ it *cannot be measured* with sufficient reliability.

Contingent asset

✓ A *possible* asset arising from *past* events ... **existence** will be confirmed only by occurrence/non-occurrence of uncertain future event(s).

2 PROVISIONS

2.1 Recognition criteria (as liabilities)

✓ All criteria must be satisfied:

   ➤ *present* obligation as result of past event;
   ➤ *probable* outflow of resources;
   ➤ *reliable estimate* can be made.

✓ Only in **extremely rare** cases will it not be possible to make a reliable estimate.

Meaning of "probable"

✓ More likely than not (i.e. greater than 50%).

2.2 Accounting treatment

Provisions **must** be recognised in the financial statements.

✓ Usually:

   Dr Profit or loss (expense)*
   　Cr Provision (liability)

* May be part of asset cost (e.g. for decommissioning).

✓ When cash is paid out to settle the liability:

   Dr Provision (liability)
   　Cr Cash (asset)

2.3 Measurement

"Best estimate" examples

✓ As evidenced by events after end of reporting period.

✓ "Expected value" (i.e. sum of possible outcomes × probabilities).

✓ Mid-point of a range of possible values.

✓ Most likely outcome (for single, "one-off" obligations).

Single obligations

✓ Must be measured *individually* (e.g. legal claims). Factors to consider:

➢ progress of claim to date;

➢ opinions of legal experts;

➢ past experience of entity in similar cases;

➢ experience of other entities in similar situations.

Large population of similar obligations

✓ Costs may be incurred frequently (e.g. product warranties).

✓ By past experience a liability can be estimated with reasonable precision.

✓ Provision is recognised when the related transactions (e.g. sales) arise ("accruals" concept).

A provision is a liability. When the obligation is satisfied any unused amount must be written back ("released") to profit or loss. It **cannot** be used for another purpose.

2.4 Disclosure (by class of provision)

✓ A reconciliation of carrying amounts.

✓ Brief description of obligation.

✓ An indication of uncertainties (amount or timing).

✓ Expected reimbursement (if any).

3 CONTINGENCIES

3.1 Nature

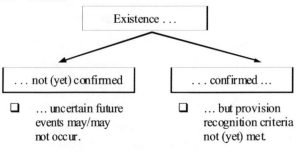

✗ Uncertainty in making an estimate does **not** characterise a contingency.

3.2 Uncertainty

✓   This can be expressed by a range of outcomes:

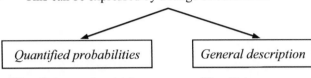

Quantified probabilities	General description

❑   Suggest a level of precision that may not be supported.

❑   Using terms – "probable" to "remote".

3.3 Contingent liabilities

✗   **Cannot** be recognised (in statement of financial position).

✓   Disclose (unless possibility of loss is remote).

✓   Recognise a provision when the loss becomes probable (i.e. no longer contingent).

3.4 Contingent assets

✗   **Cannot** be recognised ("prudence" concept).

✓   Disclose *existence* if realisation is *probable*.

✓   Recognise an asset when realisation is *virtually certain* (i.e. no contingency).

3.5 Disclosure

✓   Nature of the contingent liability/asset.

✓   Estimate of financial effect (where practicable).

✓   Uncertain factors affecting amount or timing.

4 ACCOUNTING TREATMENT

4.1 Summary

Flow of resources	Obligation	Asset
Remote	**No** disclosure	**No** disclosure
Possible	Contingent liability disclosure	**No** disclosure
Probable	Provision (if reliable estimate) – otherwise contingent liability	Disclosure required
Expected/ virtually certain	Provision	Asset (**not** contingent)

1   EVENTS AFTER THE REPORTING PERIOD

1.1   Definition

Events, both *favourable* and *unfavourable*, occurring between end of reporting period and date on which financial statements are authorised for issue.

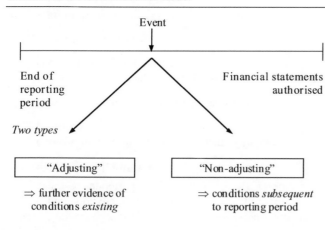

Two types

"Adjusting"
⇒ further evidence of conditions *existing*

"Non-adjusting"
⇒ conditions *subsequent* to reporting period

1.2   "Adjusting" (i.e. assets and liabilities)

✓   Further evidence assists in estimating amounts relating to conditions **existing** at the end of the reporting period.

Examples

✓   Settlement of a court case.
✓   Bankruptcy of a customer.
✓   After-date sales of inventory.
✓   Discovery of fraud or errors.

Accounting treatment

✓   Financial statements (i.e. SoFP/SoCI) are adjusted.
✓   That is, a liability (or asset) is **recognised**.

1.3   "Non-adjusting" ("Disclosing")

✓   Events of such importance that non-disclosure would affect ability of users of financial statements to make proper evaluations and decisions.

Examples

✓   Decline in market value of investments.
✓   Major acquisition/merger.
✓   Announcing a plan to discontinue operations.
✓   Destruction of assets by fire/flood.

Accounting treatment

✗   Financial statements **cannot** be adjusted (e.g. there is no liability at the reporting date).

✓   Disclosure (in the notes) is made *if material*.

1.4 Disclosure required

Date of authorisation for issue

✓ Users need to know that financial statements do not reflect events after this date.

Material non-adjusting events

✓ Nature of the event.
✓ An estimate of financial effect (or a statement that such an estimate cannot be made).

1.5 Going concern

✗ Financial statements should **not** be prepared on a going concern basis if, after the reporting period, management:

➢ intends to liquidate the entity or cease trading; or
➢ has no realistic alternative but to do so.

✓ IAS 1 requires further disclosures if:

➢ financial statements are **not** prepared on going concern basis; or

➢ there are *material uncertainties* casting significant doubt on going concern assumption.

1.6 Dividends

✓ Only dividends **declared** but not paid are a liability.

✓ Proposed *after* the reporting period but *before* the financial statements are authorised should be *disclosed* (IAS 1).

2 INTER-RELATIONSHIP WITH IAS 37

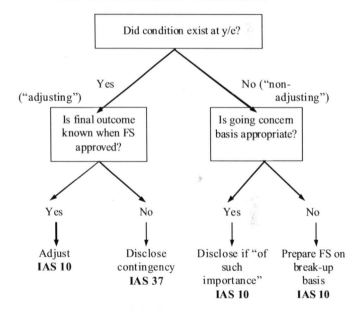

1 CASH FLOW

1.1 Cash *vs* Profits

✓ Not all profitable companies are successful; many fail through lack of cash.

✓ Profit or loss is based on accruals concept and includes non-cash items.

Function of statement of cash flows

To inform users:

✓ whether or not reported profits are being realised as cash flows;

✓ about the availability of cash to:

➢ finance investments; and
➢ pay dividends.

2 IAS 7

2.1 Scope

✓ IAS 7 applies to *all* entities.

2.2 Cash flow information

Benefits

✓ Provides information to users to evaluate changes in:

➢ net assets;
➢ financial structure;
➢ ability to affect amounts and timing of cash flows.

✓ Helps assess ability to generate cash/cash equivalents.

✓ Provides "linkage" between other financial statements.

✓ Cash is cash – eliminates effects of alternative accounting bases.

✓ Historical cash flow information may indicate future cash flows.

✓ Focus on cash management can improve results.

Drawbacks

✘ Relates to past performance.

✘ Cash position at reporting date may be "managed".

✘ Some lack of comparability:

➢ choice between direct and indirect methods;
➢ alternative classifications of interest/dividends.

✘ May be misinterpreted (e.g. net decrease in cash may not mean poor cash management).

✖ Highlighting a weak cash flow position may precipitate going concern problems.

2.3 Definitions

✓ *Cash* – cash on hand and demand deposits.

✓ *Cash equivalents* – short-term (< 3 months), highly liquid investments:

> ➢ readily convertible to known amounts of cash;
> ➢ not subject to a significant risk of changes in value.

✓ *Cash flows* – inflows/outflows of cash/cash equivalents.

✓ *Operating activities* – principal revenue-producing activities.

✓ *Investing activities* – acquisition and disposal of long-term assets and investments (excluding cash equivalents).

✓ *Financing activities* – result in changes in amount/composition of equity/borrowings.

3 PRESENTATION

3.1 Classification

Operating

✓ Generally results from transactions/events that generate profit or loss.

✓ Key indicator of sufficiency of cash flows to:

> ➢ repay loans;
> ➢ maintain operating capability;
> ➢ pay dividends;
> ➢ make new investments.

✓ Helps forecast future operating cash flows.

Investing

✓ Separate disclosure shows expenditure on resources intended to generate future income and cash flows.

Financing

✓ Separate disclosure helps predict claims on future cash flows by providers of capital/long-term finance.

3.2 Examples

Operating activities

✓ Cash receipts from:

> ➢ sale of goods/rendering services;
> ➢ royalties, fees, commissions.

✓ Cash payments to:

> ➢ suppliers for goods/services;
> ➢ and on behalf of employees.

Investing activities

✓ Payments to acquire/receipts from sales of:

➢ property, plant and equipment, intangibles;
➢ investments in other entities.

✓ Cash advances/loans (and repayments) to other parties.

Financing activities

✓ Cash proceeds from issuing:

➢ shares/equity instruments;
➢ loans, notes, bonds, other short or long-term borrowings.

✓ Cash paid to purchase own shares.

✓ Repayments of borrowings.

Interest and dividends

✓ Cash flows should be disclosed separately and classified consistently.

✓ Interest **paid**:

➢ is usually classified as *operating*;
➢ may be classified as *financing* (a cost of obtaining financial resources).

✓ Interest/dividends **received** may be classified as:

➢ *operating* (because they are included in profit or loss); or

➢ *investing* (as returns on investments).

✓ Dividends **paid** may classified as:

➢ *financing* (cost of obtaining financial resources); or
➢ *operating* (as paid out of operating cash flows).

4 OPERATING ACTIVITIES

4.1 Direct method (encouraged)

✓ Show major classes of gross cash receipts/payments:

➢ directly from *accounting records*; OR
➢ by adjusting *sales/cost of sales*.

✓ Adjustments to sales/cost of sales:

➢ changes in inventories/receivables/payables;
➢ other non-cash items;
➢ cash effects which are investing/financing.

4.2 Indirect method

✓ Adjusts *profit or loss* for effects of:

> ➢ non-cash transactions (e.g. depreciation);

> ➢ deferrals/accruals of past/future operating cash receipts/payments;

> ➢ items of income/expense relating to investing/financing cash flows.

4.3 Techniques

Direct method

Step 1	Cash receipts (from customers) Less: Cash paid (to suppliers/employees)
	⇒ Cash generated from operations.
Step 2	Payments for interest and income taxes.
	⇒ Net cash from operating activities.

Indirect method

Step 1(a)	Start with profit before tax.
Step 1(b)	Adjust for:

✓ non-cash items; and
✓ investing/financing items on accruals basis (e.g. interest).

⇒ Operating profit before working capital changes.

Step 1(c)	Make working capital changes.

⇒ Cash generated from operations (same figure as for direct method)

Step 2	As for direct method.

Proforma workings

✓ Use T a/cs to find cash flow:

Interest payable a/c

	$		$
		Bal b/f	x
Cash paid	x β	Interest charge for year	x
Bal c/f	x		
	x		x

Tax payable a/c

	$			$
			Bal b/f	x
Tax paid	x β		Tax charge for year	x
Bal c/f	x			
	x			x

Asset – Accumulated depreciation a/c

	$			$
Disposals	x		Balance b/f	x
Revaluations	x		Charge for the year	x
Balance c/f	x			
	x			x

5 INVESTING AND FINANCING ACTIVITIES

5.1 Investing

✓ Purchase of property plant and equipment:

> ➢ actual amounts *paid;*
> ➢ *exclude* trade-in/part-exchange values.

✓ Proceeds from sales of tangible assets.

Asset – Cost a/c

	$			$
Bal b/f	x			
Additions	x		Disposals	x
Revaluations	x		Balance c/f	x
	x			x

Asset – Disposal a/c

	$			$
Cost	x		Accumulated depreciation	
	x			
			Proceeds	x
Profit on sale	x		Loss on sale	x
	x			x

Exam tip! Revaluation adjustments are **not** cash flows! Cash outflow on additions will be overstated if you ignore a revaluation gain on an asset.

5.2 Financing

✓ Proceeds from issuance of share capital (includes premium paid).

✓ Proceeds from long-term borrowings.

✓ Dividends paid in the period (unless classed as operating):

   ➢ declared but not paid in prior period;
   ➢ interim dividends paid in current period.

6 COMPONENTS OF CASH/CASH EQUIVALENTS

6.1 Reconciliation

✓ Components of cash/cash equivalents presented as a reconciliation of amounts reported in the statement of financial position.

6.2 Proforma

	2013	*2012*
	$	$
Cash on hand and balances with banks	x	x
Short-term investments	x	x
	x	x

7   PROFORMA

7.1   Indirect method

Cash flows from operating activities	$	$
Profit before taxation	x	
Adjustments for:		
Depreciation [1]	x	
Investment income	(x)	
Interest expense	x	
	—	
Operating profit before working capital changes	x	
Increase in trade and other receivables	(x)	
Decrease in inventories	x	
Decrease in trade payables	(x)	
	—	
Cash generated from operations	x	
Interest paid	(x)	
Income taxes paid	(x)	
	—	
Net cash from operating activities		x

Cash flows from investing activities

Purchase of property, plant and equipment	(x)	
Proceeds from sale of equipment	x	
Interest received	x	
Dividends received	x	
	—	
Net cash used in investing activities		x

Continued	$	$

Cash flows from financing activities

Proceeds from issuance of share capital	x	
Proceeds from long-term borrowings	x	
Dividends paid	(x)	
	—	
Net cash used in financing activities		x
		—
Net increase in cash and cash equivalents		x
Cash and cash equivalents at beginning of period		x
		—
Cash and cash equivalents at end of period		x
		—

7.2   Direct method

Cash flows from operating activities

Cash receipts from customers	x	
Cash paid to suppliers and employees	(x)	
	—	
Cash generated from operations	x	
...remainder as for the indirect method		

[1] Similarly losses/(gains) on non-current asset disposals.

1 DEFINITIONS

1.1 Rule (IAS 27)

A parent must prepare **consolidated** financial statements **in addition to** its **separate** financial statements.

✓ A parent company will usually prepare its own statement of financial position (with notes) also.

  ➢ investments in subsidiaries are stated at **cost**;
  ➢ dividends are recognised when **receivable**.

1.2 Group accounts

✓ Reflect the substance of the investment.

1.3 Definitions

IFRS 10 Consolidates Financial Statement

✓ *Consolidated financial statements* – present a group as a single economic entity.

✓ *Group* – a parent and its subsidiaries.

✓ *Subsidiary* – an entity that is controlled by a parent.

✓ *Parent* – an entity that has one or more subsidiaries.

✓ *Control* – power to affect rights to variable returns.

✓ *Non-controlling interest* – **equity** in a subsidiary that is not attributable to a parent.

Non-controlling interest is a separate line item in **equity**; it is **not** a liability.

Other

✓ *Trade investment* – an investment that does not give control or significant influence (usually < 20%).

Control

✓ Owning > 50% of voting rights; or
✓ Control of the board of directors; or
✓ Majority votes at board meetings; or
✓ A legal right to govern financial and operating policies.

Significant influence

✓ Power to participate in (but not control) decision making.
✓ Gives rise to an associate undertaking.

1.4 Acquisition method (IFRS 3)

All subsidiaries must be accounted for using the **acquisition method**.

1.5 Exception to consolidation

✓ When control is **temporary** (i.e. acquired with intention of immediate resale).

2 CONCEPTUAL BACKGROUND

2.1 Substance

✓ P's "cost of investment" is replaced with:

  ➢ S's net assets (at the **end** of the reporting period); +
  ➢ goodwill (on **acquisition**).

✓ P's consolidated reserves include its share of S's **post-acquisition** reserves.

Goodwill calculation

Consideration*	X
Non-controlling interest*	X
Less: Net assets*	(X)
Goodwill at acquisition	X

* All at fair value.

2.2 Consolidation adjustments

(1) That "drive" the double entry:

  ➢ Goodwill;
  ➢ Non-controlling interest;
  ➢ Consolidated reserves;
  ➢ Fair value adjustments.

(2) Elimination of intra-group transactions and balances (including unrealised profit).

3 CONSOLIDATED STATEMENT OF FINANCIAL POSITION

3.1 Basic principles

Assets

✓ There is **no** cost of investment in S

✓ Sum **100%** of S's assets, line-by-line, with P's (regardless of P's % holding).

✓ Goodwill on acquisition is calculated on **fair values**.

Equity and liabilities

✓ Share capital = **P's only**. (Same principle applies to share premium.)

✓ Retained earnings include **P's share** of S's, **post-acquisition**. (Same principle for a revaluation reserve.)

✓ Non-controlling interest (% not owned by P) is a **separate component of equity**.

✓ Sum **100%** of S's liabilities, line-by-line, with P's (regardless of P's % holding).

3.2 Goodwill

! Goodwill is shown only in the **consolidated** statement of financial position.

! Only the carrying amount of goodwill on acquisition can be examined in F3 as "impairment" (i.e. loss in value) is **not examinable**.

3.3 Non-controlling interest

✓ Arises on a "partial acquisition".

✓ Represents that part of equity in subsidiary that is not owned by the parent.

✓ Is calculated at each **reporting date** as:

  ➤ fair value of non-controlling interest on acquisition

     plus

  ➤ non-controlling interest's share (%) of S's **post-acquisition** changes in equity.

! Only this "full goodwill" method is examinable in F3.

4 CONSOLIDATED STATEMENT OF PROFIT OR LOSS

4.1 Basic principles

✓ Sum **100%** of S's revenues, line-by-line, with P's (regardless of P's % holding). Similarly, all costs.

✓ Profit or loss is analysed between owners of the parent and non-controlling interest.

! "Other comprehensive income" is not assessed in the F3 syllabus relating to consolidated financial statements.

Illustration

P holds 75% of the voting shares of S. Bordered content is a working only (not presented).

	P	S	Consolidated
Revenue	100	10	110
Costs	(74)	(6)	(80)
Profit or loss	26	4	30

Attributable to:

Owners of the parent (26 + 75% × 4)	21
Non-controlling interest (25% × 4)	9
	30

✓ P's share = movement on post-acquisition retained earnings.

1 FAIR VALUE

1.1 Definition

The amount for which an asset could be sold (liability transferred) between market participants at the measurement date.

- ✓ A readily ascertainable market value is a fair value.
- ✓ A different transfer price is not a fair value.

1.2 Subsidiary's assets and liabilities

- ✓ Value at fair value **on acquisition** for **consolidation**.

  - ✗ This is **not** a revaluation exercise.
  - ✗ There is **no** revaluation surplus.
  - ✗ The subsidiary's books are **not** adjusted.

- ✓ Any **difference** (between fair value and carrying amount) is **adjusted** in the net asset working schedule.

- ✓ The adjustment affects the goodwill calculation.

1.3 Consideration paid

- ✓ Fair value of cash = amount of cash given.

- ✓ Fair value of own shares issued = market price of parent's shares (at acquisition date).

2 INTRA-GROUP TRADING BALANCES

2.1 Consolidated SoFP

- ✓ Parent/subsidiary balances must be eliminated on consolidation (IFRS 10).
- ✓ Current trade receivables/payables totals are reduced to reflect those of the group.
- ✓ Intra-group loans are similarly cancelled.

2.2 Consolidated profit or loss

- ✓ Intra-group sales/purchases are cancelled.

3 UNREALISED PROFIT

3.1 Consolidated SoFP

- ✓ If inventory arising from intra-group trading is held at the year end there is unrealised profit to the group.
- ✓ To eliminate, **reduce**:

  - ➤ selling company's profit (retained earnings); and
  - ➤ carrying amount of closing inventory.

- ✓ Any non-controlling interest bears its share "automatically" (on consolidation).

3.2 Consolidated profit or loss

✓ **Closing** inventory: Add unrealised profit to cost of sales of selling company (profit ↓).

✓ **Opening** inventory: Reverse prior year adjustment, assuming it has now been sold (profit ↑).

4 "MID-YEAR" ACQUISITIONS

4.1 Goodwill on acquisition

Calculate subsidiary's retained earnings at **acquisition date** assuming that **profit accrues evenly** (unless told otherwise).

4.2 Subsidiary's profits

✓ From the start of the period **up to** the date of acquisition ⇒ include in **goodwill** calculation.

✓ **After** acquisition date ⇒ include in **consolidated retained earnings** calculation.

✓ Consolidated profit or loss includes **only post-acquisition** revenue and costs.

5 INVESTMENTS IN ASSOCIATES

An entity over which the investor has **significant influence** that is not a subsidiary (or joint venture).

5.1 Significant influence

✓ Does **not** give control.

✓ Gives ability to participate in financial and operational decision making.

✓ **Presumed** to exist if investment ≥ 20% (but < 50%) of voting rights.

5.2 Equity method of accounting (IAS 28)

Consolidated SoFP

✗ Does **not** include associates individual assets/liabilities.

✓ Include a **single** asset, *investment in associate*, in non-current assets.

✓ Carrying amount is:

➢ original cost of the investment; **plus**
➢ investor's share of post-acquisition profits.

Consolidated profit or loss

✗ Does **not** include individual items of associate's revenue/costs.

✓ Include a **single** line item, *share of profit of associate*, in profit before tax.

✓ Calculated as the investor's share of the associate's profit or loss (i.e. after tax).

1 INTERPRETATION AND ANALYSIS

1.1 Involves

- ✓ Identifying users.
- ✓ Examining financial information.
- ✓ Analysis (comparison, evaluation and prediction).
- ✓ Reporting (information for economic decision-making).

1.2 Users

Internal

- ✓ To improve competitive standing.
- ✓ To identify opportunities to improve performance.

External

- ✓ Generally have access only to published financial statements.

2 RATIO ANALYSIS

The process of **determining ratios** for **meaningful comparisons** and **interpreting** them.

2.1 Purpose

- ✓ To provide a uniform measurement to indicate:
  - ➢ areas for further investigation;
  - ➢ patterns over time ("trend analysis").

- ✓ To summarise financial data into information to judge financial performance.

- ✓ Particularly useful in:
  - ➢ assessing relationships;
  - ➢ reviewing over time.

- ✓ To indicate strengths and weaknesses.

2.2 Typical comparisons

- ✓ Historical (current against previous periods)

- ✓ Actual against targets/budgets/standards.

- ✓ Against market information (other companies/industry averages, etc).

2.3 Expressing ratios

- ✓ Pure or absolute ratio.
- ✓ A rate or multiple.
- ✓ A percentage.

2.4 Interpretation

- ✓ Individual pure ratios have some but limited use (e.g. quick ratio).

- ✓ Inter-relationships between groups of ratios facilitate better interpretation.

- ✓ Historical comparisons may reveal trends over time.

✓ Caution must be exercised in making projections.

✓ Deviations from trends may identify need for corrective action.

✓ For intra-group comparisons (e.g. to benchmark performance) must adjust for different accounting policies.

2.5 Classifications

✓ By financial statement (e.g. position ratios).

✓ By nature into "primary" and "secondary" ratios.

By function

✓ Profitability:

> Gross profit %
> Net profit %
> Return on capital employed (ROCE)
> Return on Equity (RoE).

✓ Efficiency:

> Asset turnover
> Long-term asset turnover
> Inventory turnover
> Accounts receivable days
> Accounts payable days
> Working capital cycle.

✓ Liquidity:

> Current ratio
> Quick ratio.

✓ Position and stability:

> Gearing ratio
> Interest cover.

✓ Market standing.

3 PROFITABILITY

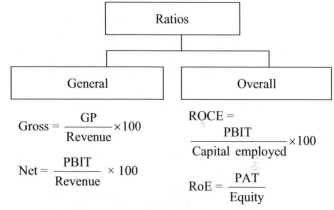

$$\text{Gross} = \frac{GP}{\text{Revenue}} \times 100$$

$$\text{Net} = \frac{PBIT}{\text{Revenue}} \times 100$$

$$ROCE = \frac{PBIT}{\text{Capital employed}} \times 100$$

$$RoE = \frac{PAT}{\text{Equity}}$$

> PBIT = Profit *before* interest and tax
> PAT = Profit *after* tax

3.1 Gross profit % (or margin)

✓ Shows the margin on each $1 of revenue.

✓ Indicates by how much selling prices may be reduced without incurring operational losses.

✓ Must be enough to cover all operational expenses, increase retained earnings and distribute dividends.

Decline may be due to:

✘ selling prices ↓ (e.g. competition ↑);
✘ unfavourable change in sales mix;
✘ purchase costs ↑ (e.g. discounts received ↓);
✘ production costs ↑;
✘ opening inventories overstated;
✘ closing inventories understated;
✓ a deliberate pricing policy (not all reasons are "bad").

Increase may similarly be due to:

✓ selling price ↑ (**without** corresponding cost ↑);
✓ costs ↓ (**without** proportionate price ↑);

3.2 Net profit %

✓ Shows overall profitability after deducting all expenses.

✓ An indicator of control over operating expenses.

✓ For further analysis calculate specific expenses (e.g. for distribution) as % of sales.

✓ Calculation may be based on profit:

➤ before investment income, interest and tax ("trading profit" margin);
➤ before interest and tax ("PBIT");
➤ before tax (i.e. after interest);
➤ after interest and tax ("PAT").

3.3 Return on capital employed (ROCE)

✓ Capital employed:

➤ is share capital + reserves + long-term liabilities (= total assets – current liabilities);
➤ may be year-end or average.

✓ Shows how productively (efficiently and effectively) available resources have been utilised, regardless of their financing.

✓ Low/falling ROCE may indicate:

➤ inefficient use of resources;
➤ a future loss if economy deteriorate;
➤ need to increase operating profit;
➤ need to sell some assets and invest proceeds for a higher return.

!	ROCE should **exceed cost of any borrowing**.

✓ Factors which may **distort** comparisons:

Over time (same entity)

➢ assets in use with negligible carrying amount ($\Rightarrow$ ROCE ↑);

➢ revaluations (capital ↑ $\Rightarrow$ depreciation ↑ $\Rightarrow$ profit ↓ $\Rightarrow$ ROCE ↓);

➢ timing of share/debt issues/redemptions;

➢ changes in accounting policies (between periods).

Between different entities

➢ different accounting policies;
➢ age of plant and equipment;
➢ leased assets not included in SoFP.

✓ Can be analysed as $= \dfrac{\text{Profit}}{\text{Revenue}} \times \dfrac{\text{Revenue}}{\text{Capital employed}}$

➢ Profit margin is a measure of *quality* of profits;
➢ Asset turnover is a *quantitative* measure;
➢ There is usually a trade-off between the two measures.

3.4 Return on equity (ROE)

✓ Equity = Ordinary share capital + reserves (year end or average)

✓ Measures residual profit against owners' investment.

✓ Shows extent to which satisfactory PAT has been achieved.

✓ Is more relevant to shareholders than ROCE.

4 LIQUIDITY – SHORT-TERM

4.1 Current ratio

✓ At end of period $= \dfrac{\text{Current assets}}{\text{Current liabilities}}$

✓ Includes all current items per SoFP.

✓ A measure of adequacy of current assets to meet short-term liabilities (without having to raise more finance).

✓ A higher ratio is normally preferable (means more liquid).

! Low/falling ratio may indicate:

✗ **overtrading**;
✗ doubts about **going concern**;
✗ undercapitalisation.

! High/increasing ratio may indicate:

- ✗ **under-trading** or **over-capitalisation**;
- ✗ **over-investment** in current assets.

✓ If going concern in doubt compare level of operating overdraft with limit of overdraft facility (if information available).

4.2 Liquid/acid test/"quick" ratio

✓ A stricter ("better") indicator of immediate solvency.

✓ Ignores least liquid asset.

✓ At period end $= \dfrac{\text{Current assets} - \text{inventory}}{\text{Current liabilities}}$

✓ Current liabilities may exclude "permanent" operating overdraft (as akin to a loan).

4.3 "Window-dressing"

"A particular type of creating accounting used to present financial statements in a more favourable light.

"Uses"

✓ To obtain funds/borrow money.
✓ To reduce tax payments.
✓ To "smooth" profits.
✓ To hide liquidity/profitability problems due to poor management decisions.

5 EFFICIENCY

5.1 Asset turnover

✓ At end of period $= \dfrac{\text{Revenue}}{\text{Total assets}}$ (no. of times)

✓ Revenue is **net** of discounts.

✓ Total assets $\equiv$ capital employed.

✓ Shows ability to use assets to generate sales (i.e. efficiency).

✓ For entities in the same industry the higher the ratio the more efficient the use of assets appears to be.

✓ If ratio declines analyse into components of assets.

5.2 Long-term ("fixed") asset turnover

✓ $\dfrac{\text{Revenue}}{\text{Non - current assets}} =$ no. of times turned per annum

✓ Show efficiency (or otherwise) in use of long-term assets.

✓ It represents revenue generated per \$1 of non-current assets.

✓ If ↓, consider disposal of surplus assets.

✓ May be distorted by revaluations (ratio ↓).

5.3 Inventory turnover/period/days inventory

✓ As no. of times $= \dfrac{\text{Cost of sales}}{\text{Inventories}^1}$

✓ Inventory period $= \dfrac{\text{Inventories}^1}{\text{Cost of sales}} \times 365$ (no. of days)

[1] Inventory may be:

➤ closing (highlights effect of major changes); or
➤ average (has dampening effect).

✓ A measure of operational and marketing efficiency.

✓ High/increasing generally indicates efficiency in selling.

*Reasons for **decrease** in turnover/increase in days*

✗ Demand ↓

✗ Poor inventory control $\Rightarrow$ costs ↑

✗ Over investment in inventory (> requirements)

✗ Holding obsolete items $\Rightarrow$ write off

✓ "Bulk" buying to obtain trade discounts

✓ "Buffer stock" ↑ to avoid costly "stockouts".

Analysis

✓ Depends on nature of business (e.g. perishable goods/contract building)

✓ In manufacturing should closely relate to production time.

✓ Higher turnover $\neq$ higher profits (as volume ↑ may be result of price ↓).

✓ Can breakdown into components (e.g. raw materials, WIP, etc).

5.4 Accounts receivable days ("collection period")

✓ As no. of days: $\dfrac{\text{Average trade receivables}}{\text{Credit sales}} \times 365$

➤ Average has "dampening" effect;

➤ Credit sales is more meaningful than total (unless insignificant cash sales);

➤ Can also calculate as no. of times.

✓ Approximation (using published financial statements):

$$\dfrac{\text{Closing trade receivables}}{\text{Sales}} \times 365$$

✓ Shows (average) time (no. of days) credit customers take to pay.

✓ If days ↑ the expense of collecting debts ↑. may be due to:

> ➢ weak credit control;
> ➢ policy to extend more credit;
> ➢ different credit terms (e.g. for major customers).

✓ Days ↓ usually good, but could flag a cash shortage.

Analysis

✓ Should be comparable with credit policy.

✓ May be negligible (e.g. supermarkets).

✓ May be distorted by:

> ➢ sales taxes;
> ➢ debt factoring;
> ➢ seasonal trading.

5.5 Accounts payable days ("average payment period")

✓ As no. of days: $\dfrac{\text{Average trade payables}}{\text{Credit purchases}} \times 365$

✓ Approximation: $\dfrac{\text{Closing trade payables}}{\text{Cost of sales}} \times 365$

✓ Shows (average) no. of days taken to pay suppliers.

✓ Days ↑ may be due to liquidity problems:

> ⇨ poor reputation;
> ⇨ withdrawal of credit and/or supplies;
> ⇨ loss of settlement discounts/penalty payments.

✓ Can be deliberate to take advantage of interest free credit.

Analysis

✓ Should be compared with "average" credit terms (e.g. on invoices).

✓ Distortion may be due to capital expenditure.

5.6 Working capital cycle

✓ No. of days = Inventory days + receivable days – payable days

✓ Shows amount of working capital needed to operate.

✓ It is the difference between current assets and current liabilities.

✓ If cycle ↑ may be due to:

> ➢ poor working capital control;
> ➢ deliberate policy (e.g. to hold more goods/extend credit to customers).

Analysis

✓ Can be negative (e.g. a supermarket) if cash received before paying suppliers.

✓ It indicates:

➢ whether cash is generated as fast as it used;
➢ cash needed to maintain operating capacity.

✓ The shorter the cycle the less reliance on external finance (e.g. overdraft).

✓ Too high means excessive interest paid/loss of interest and lost opportunities (e.g. to invest for higher return).

6 POSITION AND STABILITY

6.1 Gearing ratio ("leverage")

(a) $\dfrac{\text{Debt}}{\text{Equity}}$ (more sensitive) or

(b) $\dfrac{\text{Debt}}{\text{Capital employed}}$ $\left(= \dfrac{\text{Debt}}{\text{Debt} + \text{equity}}\right)$

✓ Debt includes long-term loans, preferred shares and "permanent" overdrafts.

✓ Equity is "residual" (ordinary share capital and reserves).

✓ Borrowed funds (for fixed return) to equity is an indicator of financial risk

✓ High gearing suits entities with relatively stable profits (to meet interest payments) and suitable assets for security (e.g. those in hotel/leisure service industry).

✓ Debt finance:

➢ is cheaper (interest is tax deductible);
➢ increases risk to shareholders (interest must be paid regardless of profit).

Analysis

✓ Preferred shares are debt if redeemable (otherwise equity).

✓ "Financial balance" means having long-term capital for long-term investments.

Overtrading

When expansion in turnover is rapid without secure additional long-term capital (i.e. **under**capitalised).

✓ Symptoms include:

➢ fast sales growth;
➢ increasing inventories/receivables/payables;
➢ decreasing cash/cash equivalents.

✓ Short-term solution: better manage working capital.

✓ Long-term solution: increase capital (share issue) or raise long-term finance.

6.2 Interest cover

Calculating

$$\frac{\text{Profit before interest}}{\text{Interest}}$$

✓ Profit before interest must also be before tax – interest is allowable expense for tax purposes.

✓ Interest amount must be expense to profit and loss: = interest paid + closing accrual – opening accrual

Analysis

✓ Indicates ability to meet interest expense out of profits generated.

✓ Interest must be paid first, even if profits fall.

! Low/falling ratio may indicate:

    ✗ potential difficulty financing debts if profits fall;
    ✗ doubts about **going concern**;
    ✗ increased risk to shareholders of falling dividends.

✗ Ratio < 2 is usually considered unsatisfactory.

7 EXAM TECHNIQUE

7.1 Which formula?

⚷ Calculate only what the information provided will allow.

✓ If no comparative information use closing balances.

✓ Use cost of goods as an approximation to credit purchases.

7.2 In a Section B question

✓ State formula used.

✓ Make concise comments:

    ➤ What does the ratio mean/show?
    ➤ What does a change mean/show?
    ➤ What is the norm (if relevant)?
    ➤ How might the change have arisen?
    ➤ What is the significance of ↑/↓ for future (i.e. implications)?

✓ Take an overview (i.e. summarise the whole picture).

ARTICLES

The following technical articles written by members of the F3/FFA examining team are available at:

www.accaglobal.com/en/student/acca-qual-student-journey/qual-resource/acca-qualification/f3.html

Examiner's report December 2016   *See next section*

IFRS 15 *Revenue from Contracts with Customers*
How to answer multiple-choice questions *
Preparing simple consolidated financial statements
Computer-based exam technique *
Trade receivables
How to prepare for Knowledge module exams *
Adjustments to financial statements

* These are listed under the "Exam Technique" section.

SPECIAL FEATURE

Examiner's guidance – see www.accaglobal.com/gb/en/student/exam-support-resources/fundamentals-exams-study-resources/f3/technical-articles/changes-to-the-structure-of-paper-f3-ffa.html

Look out for new articles published in Student Accountant www.accaglobal.com/gb/en/student/acca-qual-student-journey/sa.html.

For the full report for CBE and paper exams from July to December 2016 see: www.accaglobal.com/en/student/acca-qual-student-journey/qual-resource/acca-qualification/f3/examiners-reports.html

SECTION A

✓ The majority of candidates usually attempt questions.

✓ Candidates must:

  ➢ have a **thorough** knowledge of the **entire** syllabus;
  ➢ read the questions **carefully** and calculate any figures required before choosing a response.

This report reviews three sample Qs to give:

✓ future candidates an indication of the types of Q asked;
✓ guidance on dealing with exam questions; and
✓ a technical debrief on selected topics.

Example 1

✓ Topic: Excess depreciation transfer between reserves
✓ Syllabus area – D5(e)

Tutorial note: *The report does not comment on candidate performance but explains that it is the excess depreciation on the surplus which can be transferred each year.*

Example 2

✓ Topic: Control accounts and reconciliations
✓ Syllabus area – E3(f).

Comments

This question tested candidates understanding of the nature of errors and where corrections need to be recorded.

Example 3

✓ Topic: Suspense account
✓ Syllabus area – E5.

Comments

Tutorial note: *The report does not comment on candidate performance but explains the derivation of the balance remaining on the suspense account.*

SECTION B

✓ These questions test the preparation of:

  ➢ financial statements (including statements of cash flows) for single entities; and/or

  ➢ simple consolidated financial statements.

✓ The standard of answers was generally good.

✓ The majority attempted both questions.

Tips!

✓ Use the correct format to present your answers.
✓ Know how to apply various accounting techniques.
✓ Present neat and logical workings.
✓ Clearly state answer to any MCQs in this section.

December 2016

How candidates may improve their performance (* denotes paper-based exams):

Q1: Consolidation statement of financial position

✓ Read the information provided carefully.

✓ Remember, markers **can** only give "method" marks for incorrect amounts if **workings** are **shown**.*

Tip! Small workings can be done "on the face" of an answer. Separate workings **must** be cross-referenced!

✓ Give appropriate title (e.g. "Consolidated statement of …. at [date]").*

✓ Use the correct format – there is usually 1 mark for presentation.*

✓ Assets and liabilities of the parent and subsidiary are added together on a line-by-line basis.

✓ Investment in subsidiary is replaced with goodwill.

✗ Do **not** add share capital and share premium balances.

✓ Adjust receivables and payables for any intra-group balances and eliminate.

✓ Adjust inventory for any unrealised profit.

Q2: Statement of profit or loss for a single entity

✓ Carefully read the information provided.

! Not everything given in a trial balance will be needed.

✓ Read any notes to identify adjustments or calculations required (e.g. prepayments or accruals).

✓ Use the correct format (i.e. IAS 1) showing total distribution costs and total administrative expenses. There is usually one mark for format/presentation. *

✓ Calculate depreciation using the stated method.

✓ Show workings and reference them. *

Give correct title to the financial statements.

Comments relating to CBE exams (June 2014 report)

Read the question **carefully** and **follow the instructions**. For example:

✓ some questions specify $000 or $m;

✓ others instruct to ignore brackets or signs when entering negative numbers.

Warning! If a pro-forma answer shows a line as "Less: xxx", **no** minus sign or brackets should be put round the figure as "Less" already indicates that it is negative.

In statement of cash flows questions, **all** figures should be entered with **no** minus sign or brackets – the drop down list must be used to indicate whether the amount is positive or negative.

Conclusions

✓ Care must be taken in reading each "stem".

✓ The syllabus/subject areas cannot be learnt "by rote".

✓ Question practice is essential to understanding topics so that knowledge can be applied to **any questions** presented.

✓ Use the Specimen Exam* as a guide to:

➤ styles of questions;

➤ coverage of topics;

➤ approximate split between calculation and non-calculation questions.

---

* See www.accaglobal.com/gb/en/student/exam-support-resources/fundamentals-exams-study-resources/f3/past-pilot-papers.html for the CBE specimen and related resources.

General

✓ Allocate your time. On average:

  ➢ 2-mark MCQs ≈ 2½ minutes
  ➢ 15-mark MTQs ≈ 18 minutes

✓ Answer all questions.

Multiple choice questions (MCQs)

✓ MCQs mostly consist of:

  ➢ a "stem" (the question)
  ➢ a "key" (the correct answer)
  ➢ 3 "distracters" (plausible but incorrect answers).

✓ Some 1-mark MCQs have only 2 distracters or are "true/false" type.

Exam tips

✓ Double entry skills will be tested on, for example:

  ➢ correction of errors
  ➢ journal entries
  ➢ ledger control accounts
  ➢ bank reconciliations.

✓ Cover up answers A, B, C, D while making calculations.

✓ When time is up, guess! But avoid the least plausible-looking answer (e.g. a disproportionate amount).

Multi-task questions (MTQs)

✓ Read requirement(s) carefully and highlight "instruction" and "content".

✓ **Remember**: For longer Qs (and parts thereof) the first marks are easiest so **always** move on to next Q when time allocation is up.

✓ Financial statements (or extracts):

  ➢ may be for any entity (sole trader, incorporated or consolidated).

✓ In paper-based exams:

  ➢ Set out a clear pro-forma with relevant captions (only);

  ➢ Use a columnar layout;

  ➢ Show all workings and cross-reference;

  ➢ NEVER "finish" or "tidy up" when time is up.

Non-computational questions

✗   Do not write an essay!

✓   Jot down relevant ideas on an answer plan.

✓   Use subheadings to address what is being asked for.

✓   Bullet points (but **not** "note form") are easiest to mark.

✓   Work to 1 mark per relevant point clearly made.

✓   "Explain …"

  ➤   Give justification
  ➤   Define terms
  ➤   Use illustrations or examples.

Presentation

✓   Is **important** in paper-based exams!

✓   Use **only black** ink.

✓   Use headings, subheadings and underline with a ruler.

✗   Do **not** use liquid paper.

✓   Show all workings and cross-reference.

✗   Do **not** underline "key words"

ABOUT BECKER PROFESSIONAL EDUCATION

Becker Professional Education provides a single solution for students and professionals looking to advance their careers and achieve success in:

- Accounting
- International Financial Reporting
- Project Management
- Continuing Professional Education
- Healthcare

For more information on how Becker Professional Education can support you in your career, visit www.becker.com/acca.

Substantially derived from content reviewed by ACCA's examining team

BECKER
PROFESSIONAL EDUCATION®